Praise for *This Household of Earthly Nature*

Dear Reader, prepare thyself to burst. *This Household of Earthly Nature* is a hard-won, grief-sown celebration. This is our emergency: "the crush of angels...the electric hymnal of the night." In language such as this, the world as we encounter it appears too beautiful and full of grief, too irreversible and headlong bearing down to think and feel beyond the incandescent limits of our attention. Part paean to the fact-lit materia of creation, part elegiac song of loss, the single poem that is this book unfolds as a kind of spiral litany, a keeping track of things at once in deep relation and beset upon by cosmic loneliness. Here, for you, are the stark occurrences of a writer's earth-bent wrack-line vision.

—Nick Gulig, poet laureate of Wisconsin

Cody-Rose Clevidence demonstrates, in a sprawling network of erudition that is itself a materialist testament to ordinary beauty and an experimental synthesis of poetry and science, that knowledge is remediated half and afterlives, that nature is as we have done, and love, that invisible force that truly connects us, by necessity coagulates with information, infrastructure, instantaneity, and other ineluctable lows that humanity won't be here much longer to witness. *This Household of Earthly Nature*'s anti-prescriptivist contradiction, and generative genius, is that its operations it no other model than Clevidence's own anarchic making, one which would share and encompass everything we've ever made.

—Alicia Wright

This Household of Earthly Nature

This Household of Earthly Nature

an essay: a year, a life, a country, a global network

Cody-Rose Clevidence

ISBN: 979-8-9915011-6-3
Library of Congress Control Number: 2025936446

Book design by Holly Melgard
Editor: James Sherry

Acknowledgments: Many thanks to the editors of journals where some of this work first appeared; *Gulf Coast*, Brian Teare for *Poem-a-Day*, *Peripheries*, and Green Linden Press's anthology *Essential Queer Voices of U.S. Poetry*.

NEW YORK STATE OF OPPORTUNITY | Council on the Arts This book is made possible, in part, by the New York State Council on the Arts with the support of the office of the Governor and the New York State Legislature.

Roof Books
are published by Segue Foundation
300 Bowery Fl 2
New York, NY 10012
seguefoundation.com

Roof Books are distributed by
Independent Publishers Group
For book orders, please go to IPGbook.com

"Thy limitless crops, grass, wheat, sugar, oil, corn, rice, hemp, hops / Thy barns all fill'd, the endless freight-train and the bulging storehouse, / The grapes that ripen on thy vines, the apples in thy orchards, / Thy incalculable lumber, beef, pork, potatoes, thy coal, thy gold and silver, / The inexhaustible iron in thy mines."

—Walt Whitman, *Leaves of Grass*

*

"For whatever we do today in physics- whether we release energy processes that ordinarily go on only in the sun, or attempt to initiate in a test tube the processes of cosmic evolution, or penetrate with the help of telescopes the cosmic space to a limit of two and even six billion light years, or build machines for the production and control of energies unknown in the household of earthly nature, or attain speeds in atomic accelerators which approach the speed of light, or produce elements not to be found in nature, or disperse radioactive particles, created by us through the use of cosmic radiation, on the earth— we always handle nature from a point in the universe outside the earth. Without actually standing where Archimedes wished to stand, still bound to the earth through the human condition, we have found a way to act on the earth and within terrestrial nature as though we dispose of it from outside, from the Archimedean point. And even at the risk of endangering the natural life processes we expose the earth to universal, cosmic forces alien to nature's household."

—Hannah Arendt, *The Human Condition*

*

"From pyramids to cathedrals to football matches, history is the story of so much energy, money, time and blood spent on so many activities that involve thinking of a world beyond.... I don't look at the metaverse as some new thing we're doing. We're just building another cathedral."

— Some Guy about the internet on the internet

*

"In 1934, after considering the senses of ticks, dogs, jackdaws, and wasps, Jakob von Uexküll wrote about the Umwelt of the astronomer. 'Through gigantic optical aids,' he wrote, this unique creature has eyes that 'are capable of penetrating outer space as far as the most distant stars. In its [Umwelt], suns and planets circle at a solemn pace.' The tools of astronomy can capture stimuli that no animal can naturally sense—X-rays, radio waves, and gravitational waves from colliding black holes. They extend the human Umwelt across the extent of the universe and back to its very beginning."

—Ed Yong, *An Immense World: How Animal Senses Reveal the Hidden Realms Around Us*

*

"Attitudes toward historical change will be found only occasionally in writings ostensibly devoted to 'history' and often have to be read into such writings. They must also be read into sagas and epics, sacred scriptures, funerary inscriptions, glyphs and ciphers, vast stone monuments, documents locked in chests in muniment rooms, and marginal notations on manuscript."

—Elizabeth Eisenstein, *The Printing Press as an Agent of Change*

*

"That hellish world, devoid of grace—has it arrived?"

—James Gleick, *The Information*

*

"The prairie's sweep is flat infinity,
The cities rise is perpendicular to farthest star,
I stand where the two directions intersect,
In any town or county in the land,
Level with my fellow men,
Right-angled to the universe"

—Jean Toomer, "The Blue Meridian"

I dedicate to the visible world

[O] undergirded world, built thing, sing—you miles of conduit, incandescent lacework of nanosecond wires and wireless internet servers overheating in the desert—here we are—here we are hurtling along—here, we are—satellites of time's weird tabernacle—among the once plowed farm-field-ten-thousand-acre-blastocyst-and-ova of Super-Megalopolis America interstate highway system strip mall box store dominion; walk with me along these 7-dimensional streets at all the intersections of this tiered and quilted and beautiful country, while the milky-way wheels overhead. there are shadows cast on the avenue walls; the coverage map catches us all in its now-vibrating net. the rain is coming from the west or are those fires. there are rivers of light cast out upon the freeway. some idiot deity has spilled these sparks across the universe, and what have we done with it. something is leaking at the seams. the frayed wires strain in the Mobius circuit as our soul does. come with me through the fiber-optic nerve bundles, the 5G-hyperreal muscle-cord cables of this our shared hive, electric mind, a thousand wormholes tunneling from our fingertips, mating birds quantum signaling across the ionized surface, rock dust, particles hurtling through us. we are secreting our glittering data across the vast expanse, all together, now—

that the world exists. that the net amount of water for the world exists from microbe to tidal pool to first irrigation ditch, lung and metabolism of a habitable planet, net amount of water for a country, microplastics and heat death in the long duration. prerequisite for a food chain: water, movement, desire; the first glucose of the first fruits; cell wall, sugar-ratio, sunlight. vinegar [to] wine. holy font [my] catechism. flies, gather.   it will be a celebration.

all together now, we will call it folding.
abate, barometric pressure!   let up off us

open all the gates   let go the tempo to the soil
one for ancestors   one for ghosts

as fear relates to prayer
vinegar to vine

as fear relates to prayer   to keep it in your memory, yes
knowing only memory is a vessel

knowing memory is only a vessel   in which things
change to other things   ancestors to kings
the viaduct of souls in the long procession

don't take the prayers down into your own mind—you alligator of the
deep—they will change   and like all things   become unforgivable

the prayer's a rusted thing that has its broken axle in us   in us the
whinnying of the horses   the plumes   the gear ratio of heaven's
mouth to heaven's hooves   our excess exhaust's hot breath's hallelujahs
polluting this once blue—   twice blue—   sky

carcinogen-hallelujah.   it is true.
we already won   this is heaven
are you happy, here?

REAL BEEF 2 for $6 how much did you, Arby's, pay for the whole
tender-eyed long-lashed knobby-kneed bovine baby born bleating
somewhere—Ohio? Panama? warm palm-sized parcels of the universe
loved by a mother-mammal once, probably—chemical-induced sensation of
motherly love—social-mammal-kinship selection sensation—honed-over
evolution's millennia, eons, mammalian aspect of a child's pure
unadulterated terror bleak field of what's left of earth : [ratio of] fuel
costs shipping containers ethanol refrigeration containers on freight
tracks through the desert west Texas Montana [...] flowers in the
fields of someone's ancestors—but whose? and where are they now?

raw materia filtered light still-standing orchard or grove or underpass

tent city the tanks are coming finger-print scanning lock black
box of the stolen universe's desire for itself protection racket of
the universe and all the skies of the multiverse heaving out new stars so
dance

this maddening rhyme galloping somewhere in the optical illusion which is
a city the city of man metropolis humans or ants in the storehouse of
heaven

> Wes Jackson writes, in *Altars of Unhewn Stone*, of "advances in modern agriculture"—implies that this has all been "the fall" since the first drainage ditch, the first irrigation canal that we built and shaped our world to inhabit us, the first tended seed brought in from the cold, covered, gently, watered, gently, the longest, slowest fall.

what is a blessing, really? after all?

pour one out, for me tillage of lettuce rows of the universe
till each nerve ending on earth

to us the world
[what is or isn't shared]

what is or isn't shared: it's not nothing, actually. unfortified city 5-
gigabyte videos of dinosaurs streamed from the Smithsonian Museum
answer of a billion billion trillion quadrillion beings, functional infinities of
bugs, quiet moss, air-flight-control data maps in "real-time" short
window of our own consciousness, loves, and over there, standing tall,
shrouded Death with her hourglass and scythe in the ethanol field:
sunflowers, sunflowers, sunflowers all.

what is or isn't shared and who you share it with corn planted out
with robotic arms in endless rows marching toward the sunset
to sit down to eat with your family if you have that. a small repetitive task—
ritual kinship of every living thing "we are calling to ask you about your
car's extended warranty" bless me in the sepulcher and let the cool night air
wring a few more hallelujahs out of me from gas pump to gas tank
from sea to shining other sea. touch with your imaginary mind each soul or
sentient spark in the fertilized eons that have gone before that may or
may not come after pour one out for them this is their world we live
inside they built it for us boat on the lake of our soul they who
invented the wheel the well pump the family unit silicon valley zero
the backyard grill the totem emblem symbol and sign the wireless
telephone the microchip prayer oil refinement
chemotherapy the calculations of the orbits of the stars—

a telescope of time's dominion
genetic lineage of each seed

whatever will be our legacy in the long continuation
how rapidly the earth will grow back over the place where we had been
once, just molecules rearranging endlessly on the green football field of time

as fear relates to prayer   mercy has an idle breast, migrates
north in summer, heat raise up off the pavement, sunset in the Lowe's
parking lot, sunset around the globe, a continuous thing. it sets for me over
the Lowe's parking lot just behind the giant LOWE'S sign, neon blue against
the sky pink and darker blue, then slides to Chris and Sara in Boise, then to
Jane and Opal in California, then into the ocean for a while. in the morning
of this hemisphere after it has slid across the surface of another deep cold
ocean, it will break over the side of the world to my mother on the eastern
seaboard, and she will start her day again. when I was little, I used to have
dreams there were giant sharks in that ocean just under the surface, circling.
and there are. helicopters fly up and down the coast, tracking them.
mercy moves north with the tides.

the algae that blooms blooms in our collective mind.
the helicopters that whir whir in our collective mind.
the traffic jams that stretch into the sunset stretch
into the sunset. the great falcons still nest on the taiga, the osprey
on telephone poles. we hatch fish in fish hatcheries and stock them
in all the rivers and lakes of America.

the golden arches : conglomerate : how many different cows in one fast food
hamburger : amalgam of how many souls : grey meat paste of many souls

and why would anyone want to be just one soul, walking across the universe?

there is no such thing as a single soul [or] there is no such thing as the universe.

think about the genetic mutations in a pineapple
think about the cost of a pineapple
think about the land cleared for farms
and the networks of roads and highways and shipping lanes
used to transport inputs, like fertilizer, and outputs like pineapples
think of each hand and what else those hands touch every day, children,
dishes, genitals, phones, machine-fabricated parts
of our built world, door handle,
subway rail, credit card, ritual objects of daily motions, daily
objects of ritual motion, coffee mug, asphalt, gas nozzle,
phone charger, outlet, these are the blessings
we have to say if we want the world to be beautiful
as it is not as it was in our imagination

[one question is to what extent the planet has a metabolism, can *heal itself* after a catastrophic event—to what extent the biosphere constitutes a macro living system. *at what unit of measurement* is a system considered *alive.* [for example] over half the DNA biomass of our own bodies are not "our own" but we consider ourself to be one organism. each scale has its lens in which meaning is a functional arrangement at each scale and can be scaled up or down to reveal different processes.]

Kentucky coal mines, Pittsburgh steel
pipe manufacturing, porcelain
toilet industry, history
of mental illness, divine
inspiration, seed
capital, nest
egg, bible
belt, go
west, clever
girl, a "sense
of wonder"
in Roanoke
they ate each other, to go
in one direction
then another—weave
weft, warp, fibers
of memory, lineage
a net:

Kierkegaard:
"the self is a relation
that relates itself to its own self"

the meaning-making mind makes meaning,
holds out the empty cup of air and pours, feels
an echo in our deep bell, ascribes—

prayer = pattern making + social animal
kinship, dominion of all things, connectedness
of all things—in our mind, in our mind's eye

what is the braid of history through time
and what do we need to do to maintain it
the ties that bind, ancestor worship, son of man, son
of which terrible god, which minor deity's house or
clan, king lists, made-world in the image of passage,
lineage is not divinity, empty ceremony of meaning-
making, primal wound, mother, country, brainstem,
testicle and anklet of god, so eat

solar power & planned obsolescence : musical notes disintegrating in
saturated air

"we sowed salt into the fields, that they could not grow" TOP TEN RESILIENT FOOD CROPS FOR A HOTTER FUTURE : *"free shipping"* from the past, to now.

times arrow & life's desire for itself
if there are a hundred million seeds
if there is one drop of rain
if there is a net amount of force
if there is a season then there will be
a flood   there will always be something next
of that you can   rest   assured

we just won't be here to see it
from our spaceships in the outer orbit
"endless forms most beautiful"
prosciutto pink and thin sliced from the store
you can be happy, here

some things hold steady   the effect of war on global commodity
prices   the sensation of missing someone   the mammal need for
gentle or playful touch   the expansion rate of the universe   hear me
architects of the viaducts   geneticists of a future race   the apples
need to be bitterer   we have to use our muscles
in active engagement with the world   or we will lose it
lose it all : muscle, engagement, world. sense-bombardment frays attention
and attention is a muscle

"to understand the universe we'd need a life-size model of it," Carl Sagan
says. "Luckily," he says, "we already have one"

so make your microchip-brained computers sing in the void   now we will
build some new relation   with this young dumb thing electric that has its
hold of us.

be gentle with us at it   weird new cathedral
teach us how to worship   how to unlock the next level
in the game the universe is playing with itself

we are new here in the multiplied universe
and the portal to the world is very small
and getting smaller
and we are falling backwards
off of it

[today] I clear rocks and watch the squash bugs
eat the squash leaves in my garden, yellow with
black spots, or the red aphids, the assassin bugs
or the long blister-beetles, or the squash-borer larvae
that root into the base of the root-stalk and wilt
the whole plant from the heart of it.

god – the caterpillars
damn – in wonder
god – the pesticides of this
greenest eden
Dam – the river, the army corps
of engineers built the water-
supply reservoir for the city, so that you
can take a shower, wash your dishes
hum yourself a little song

restricted water allotment for lawns, Los Angeles, the states vying for water-rights on the Colorado, almonds, citrus, I love lemons, dry eyes of the angel, grimace of the million-lunged god of engines, traffic jam on the sunset of the idols, bless.

5 burgers for 7 bucks and a blue Gatorade, after we come back from fishing below the hydroelectric dam where the catfish aren't biting, and the barges make their way upriver, and the Tyson Turkey plant pumps out its waste into the wide rolling brown Arkansas downstream.

the coming storm: "whoever makes that great brown river smile"

the fortified garden, the fatty membrane – the truth is somewhere in there – in all that tangle there – sanctuary, care – effluvia and pollutants and rivers and trash stuck in tangled briars, razor-wire of the enclosed garden, metropolis, a precious thing, evolved lifeways, the mitochondria are the powerhouse of the cell sweet land of liberty:

"I lift" "my lamp" "and sing"

sweet mercy; suicide rates of eden; the hospitals are all named mercy; Janus of opposites; freedom to wear the blue dress in Ohio, freedom to be whole and inviolate in one's own skin, to touch gently the universe of forms and come back different and more thoughtful, to make new choices in the flowing data-stream, to give up or to try again, freedom to drive to Tulsa in sunlight, to pay the price of gas, to not get pulled over going over the speed limit, ratio of colleges to prisons in a country, how much we pay prison workers in America, the eggs are 4.99, the cotton shirt is 9.99, this is the mechanical loom, this is the human know-how, this is the ratio of love to loss, what is it to live a good life, each to tend one's own corner of the galaxy, "freedom is always self-determination" I tell my nazi neighbor, "you don't get to decide someone else's freedom, you can only listen." "*under conditions of complete liberty*" Adam Smith writes over and over again, first premise never realized. hold the world open for everyone, skyscrapers or tall grass prairie, trash filled creek and small-town gas station

of thee
I sing.

what else could be a blessing.

pour one out for us.

today the ground is parched in Arkansas

irrigation systems, the first step out of the wilderness
to grow where it cannot grow; what is most human in us

that we dig and flood   that there are dangers
that there are joys   what we want to protect

how we conceive of protecting them

how we carry them with us into the future
long gestation period, saved seeds, vestige and symbol of family or home

a cell wall forms a barricade that protects the inner metabolism from
establishing equilibrium with what's outside

collective labor   kinship rituals   sanctuary   refuge

chaos as in thermodynamics and chaos as in violence
rootedness [in what relation to] flux

an actual garden for each person on earth   how else could we eat

the constant tending that keeps this entropic flood at bay, what is *necessary*,
what is *sufficient*, what is *joyful*, what is *lossless*, what is *grief-at-the-never-ending-flow-of-time*, what is *the best we can do with the resources available to us*

"we sowed salt into the fields, that they could not grow"

I hear the birdsong change when my cat goes outside

stacking stones   the art of weaving.
a sudden fervor came upon them.

architect. archetype. viaduct & sewer commissioner board bless   men who have blest other men   permission to live amongst you   permission to grow grain   to modify the corn   to cultivate a blue flower for your soul which is my soul and all the souls of men.

permission to build the greatest city on earth, permission to build an internet, permission to launch satellites across the night sky, like this, permission to mine silica, salt, uranium, iron, coal, bless, permission to drive on the rutted and crumbling highways of America, permission to zoom in on google maps: The Grand Canyon, The Great Lakes, The Mississippi River, The Big Apple, The Rocky Mountains, Cincinnati, bless. what wind blows today; where does the rain fall; what is the price of gas? crude oil pumped through miles of conduit, regalia of factions, razorback stadium, insignia & pride flag, bless. "I'm sorry I made a mistake," the tweet reads. "it's my first time being alive." O ungod, please take us all [out].

(back ?)   to the paradise ?   city ?   where the grass is green ?   and the girls –

what freedom is. humans are always dancing; juvenile humans love to dance.

chronicler of my amazement: tell me   in the long
lineage and biodome of thought, tell me   cursory glance at the
world, visible [to us] color-spectrum, microscopic things in every orifice, tell
me, how far can we go?   steel-beamed tower up to heaven   paradox
of a blue globe hard crusted earth and us before it   get dressed up   go
to a friend's party   ride the elevator   a friend who you love   who
you have known for a long time now   savor a small
moment, before   a small moment, after

we come bearing gifts—

porcelain toilet of our orbit   canonical
diagram of civilizations, hear me   mine own
one squeak, anthem in the rushing wind   vowels of the self-same world
as always   O my palindrome dome-of-triumph remote-
controlled-drone missiles of this mine and or other countries Missile Defense
Shield System, firewall, paywall   the walls to the city were
15ft thick   the fortifications included six chambers   like that of the wasp-
killing spider   nest-egg   hear me here for just this one hum of the wires
hoarse syllabics of the first vowels   song crushed into the first grapes—

fold the beauty down in the racket of
hold the beauty deep in the socket of
fold the ordinary down in the whole expanse of
halt the crane in its tracks the 4-lane highway
where I opened my error up and stepped over
the ordinary beauty of the down-bolted world

to bring food to a hospital, hawk tearing apart a squirrel in the city park,
gather

it will be a celebration.

and how many died on the rooftops of their city, Uruk. to escape the heat, shade tree & pavement, public fountain the kids play in, the cooling centers set up in every major city, heat desert and food desert and the necessary apparatus of living in all the places we have chosen to live, we have made possible to live, where we have forced people to live. take a shit in all the golf course holes for me. the air conditioning hums in my cabin in Arkansas, the insulation visible between roof-joists where the wrens make their nests in spring. I charge the car-battery in my Chevrolet with a drip-charger plugged in to an extension cord plugged into the Ozarks Electric Cooperative power pole as the dew condenses on blades of grass, the leaves of the mulberry trees, the small fig-tree cutting from a fig Carson's grandfather brought over "on the boat" and which her mom propagated for me in Greenville, Mississippi. the sky rolls again over us. I think of eggplants grown in the first gardens, bitter flesh, potential seeds, the future, hands.

permission to order silk pillowcases on the internet
permission to buy the bright green shoots bundled at the grocery store
permission to buy dish soap and bug spray and vinegar, butter and retinol face-cream and the translucent flesh of a fish from some shining ocean somewhere. caught in some shining net somewhere, hauled in by some shining hands somewhere.

net amount of violence in the garden, net acreage of the garden, net amount of knowledge that has ever been known. the work that maintains the edges of that. Walmart-Archipelago down the lighted corridors of our soul, a feeling of helplessness—3 romaine hearts in a plastic bag, stacked, harvested at night in Southern California's "inland empire," permission for the lettuce to be bigger, greener, permission to discard the outer layers on heavens threshing floor, permission to sit down in the shade in the heat of the day. high noon of the idols. slugs in a cup of rain. a sense of instability at all the edges, getting closer.

permission to pump crude oil through the tribal lands, permission to pump petroleum though neighborhoods whose mean income is below the national poverty line, they own the trailers but they don't own the land the trailers are on, permission to put up a Dollar General there, permission to pump gas for $4.55 a gallon at the EZ-Mart, permission to buy a yellow energy drink, "tropical" flavor, permission to swim in the rivers, permission to swim in the lake that is the water for the city, permission to piss in the lake that is the water for the city, permission to fish in the lake that is the water for the city, permission to read the sign that is only in English that is a warning about mercury levels in the fish, permission to blast out the oil from under Oklahoma, Montana, Kansas, permission to graze cattle there. now there are earthquakes. the algae blooms in the fertilizer runoff. the small marine animals make a home on the floating islands of trash

O Langston what have we done to your rivers, the pluroflourocarbons in the rainwater joyride around the globe, the water cycle that is the metabolism of a habitable planet, the sewage wastewater treatment plants sing on the wide rolling rivers, oil slicks glitter their myriad and pulsing rainbows on the great writhing surface, electricity chants through the power grid, each to each, spill one over for us, joules heaped upon joules, children swim in the rivers, old men fish in the rivers, old men fish under the overpass in the city park, nightcrawler earth worms $2.99 for 4oz at the gas station where you can get fried catfish, BBQ, two 8oz redbulls for $5 and pure, clear, liquid gasoline right out of the pump.

it is hot, it is summer, children swim
in incandescent blue blow-up
swimming pools on irrigated green lawns

the dried up river reveals fossil footprints
of children playing in Pleistocene mud

"all kids like to play in muddy puddles"
the article says, the casting of nets,

aggregate knowledge,
and what we want to protect.

each steps in and takes their turn touching
the endless bowstrings of the braid of time,

the time that flows as a river around us and through us
one by one we pass on into the history of the universe

we will weave the earth this dress of time which will outlast us, whatever remains will not remember us, though, sure, all molecules go into the long continuation—"the smallest sprout shows there is really no death." No, that is not my prayer, Walt Whitman. it doesn't comfort me. when I speak, slowly, I want the universe to listen. permission to pierce the vacuum of space with our golden needle-arrow missive sailing outward, permission to record our human voices singing, saying hello in a thousand languages, permission to draw our human bodies naked, to come down from the trees, permission to dress up in plumage and colors, permission to bear witness, permission to structure violence in less damaging ways, ritual-dance, football, bake-offs, permission to build the atheneum, the Thunderdome, the viaduct, permission to kneel down in the shower in the fluorescent light, the Bluetooth speaker keening softly in the other room searching for its connection. I watch the moon come up over the rise of the next hill and take a picture with my smartphone. the dinosaurs were sentient; they lived here for 200 million years.

to take things out of the entropic flow of time, what writing is, to outsource to your environment durable information, of which memory is the first flicker, first rung of the ladder up, to carry a thought over into the future, to exist (momentarily) outside of time, notation scratched in dust, on a cave wall, daily notches on a bone mark 28 days, a pressing concern, first knowledge known first.

memory, which is the material aspect of time,
the chemical reactions that are the flow of time
relation: vinegar to wine

when you learn the constellations of your culture: how the stars arrange
themselves, coalesce into forms, form signs, progress in a set delineation,
which is an arrow toward "the future" which is the spiral arm of that galaxy,
which is the spiral arc of time and what on earth will happen next?

this world where plastics swirl
in the churning gyre of the churning seas, bless
the heatwave coming in from the west. net
eye of storm, now here, now there, net
amount of water on earth.

my friends, who I love
in Louisiana, walking their dogs
at the bad-dog levee while storm
cells gather over the warm and
warming water of the Gulf,
the Pearl River rising on the coasts,
footage of houses falling into the surf,
in Arizona, footage of fires,
stories on the radio, my friends are going
out tonight in Brooklyn, Amelia
is playing a show at the Jalopy,
people are going out to eat, going
to the movies, Mickey
is catching fish in Alaska, Dallin
is growing weed in Oklahoma, Sara
got a new job teaching in Boise,
my mother is well taken care of
and as happy as she's ever been,
Timmy is moving to Philadelphia,

we are going to read *Kapital* together,
Jane is depressed but persevering,
Haeree is driving to Cheyenne in the
meteor shower, Alexia and I drink wine
on Zoom, the gas prices are falling again,
I plant my corn and look out through
my rectangular hell portal of the universe
at the news, NOAA data, radar, patterns, maps
I raise my glass to us—

my water is getting low in my catchment tanks.
I plant my corn like little teeth and try to feel a lineage
to all of human history, and further,

the article says "400 billion dollar plans for a new city in the desert" — "former Walmart executive" named, ironically, Ozymandias — who built the Memphis Bass Pro Shop's Pyramid, who hauled asphalt for the endless parking lots of eden, still shining heart of my country, from trash-filled sea to trash-filled sea "to be spiritualized by a new America." O Jean Toomer I carry your torch in my pocket, it is a camera too and doom portal, and I hold it up to the great face of Being and take pictures of ordinary things, a tiny moon in the night sky, a pickle at the Brooklyn Botanic Garden, a hydroelectric factory glittering grey on a grey lake by the highway in Kansas, my dog rolling on his back in the sun in the dirt in the yard, a cool green and gold beetle I haven't seen before. would that we could wake up all together in some shining futuretropolis on the banks of some great brown river smiling electric with eels, with green rushes and migrating fish and a distant sound of music or a highway or some as-yet hopeful construction, raise up the cranes, raise up our shining glass, glowing gold in the light, clinking ice from somewhere, watch the great blue herons catch fish, migrate, we could name Memphis after Memphis, as if we had souls, as if our souls continued on in the long continuance, eat our breakfast all together on this new morning of the new world.

no.

cities built into the cracking hillsides, cities stacked up overlooking the sea, cities incrementally crusting outward like tree rings from central waterways, port-city bypass highways, tunnels, bridges, balustrades, minarets, stone-arch and glass and plexiglass and shining metal spires. some new material, this is the space age window's steel beams, cities as geometric crystalline foam thrust up from the ocean hexagonal chambers piled high on cliffs sparkling in the light, cities glowing like heaps of embers at night scattered across the dark land turning into and out of the sun, cities radiating outward as lichen on rocks, cities accreting like sores on the desert, quarries seen from above in time-lapse blooming, reaching branching tendrils creeping up coasts along arterial highway systems, intricate lacework electrical tangle and maze, cities shining in the haze from sea to shining human hive the throbbing heart of the network.

1000 howitzers and 1000 drones   steel and lace
a place, a face, a name   many names

brainstem   violence   lizard   shame
build up the shining cathedral, mote in the eye of
the eye of the storm. come cumulus, trigonometry, come
apex and cosine, come stand before me, amalgam
of organisms, shape of thought shaped, eon, reaction,
generation, futility of prayer—the hummingbird hawk moth,
the iridescent blue swallowtail, tomato horn worm, whole lives
lived once, in the glittering air of each empire, momentous
moment in a moment suspended, whole. I kill the giant horseflies, step
on the hornworms, buy insecticide to kill the aphids and mosquitos, the leaf-
cutter bugs, and squash-borer beetles, etc. I plant milkweed for the orange
monarchs on their great migrations, leave the fishing spiders alone, & order
lacewing larvae online. in short, I am a tiny god.

we all make our choices in the universe.

what are the conditions that bring out violence
where is the location of belonging
what is the structure of the nature of human thought
the relationship; tools : thumbs

my neighbors say, "we might not even have a country soon." the fall of civilizations podcast narrator says, "let us imagine what it would have been like to live in this time...." the meme on the internet says, "every evening I pinch the bridge of my nose and remind myself that millions of people led full and satisfying lives during the collapse of the roman empire." the YouTube population-data tracker shows a glowing dot for every one million people across the surface of the globe since 40,000 bce; it starts slow, each little glowing dot and chime, a blip, a different blip, now here, now there, now moving north, east, west, blip, blip, then faster, blip blip blip, spreading out over all the continents, little starbursts of light, contagious, blipblipblipblip, coalescing, all at once; now it crescendos, explodes with thousands of dots and chimes all over lapping, in bright clusters everywhere, growing brighter, gone supernova, bursting its seams, whole continents, over all. I think "like fish roe." my friend says, "like doom pop-rocks."

go forth in amazement; this world we have made

Interstate Highway System, central air, reservoir 200 miles from the city. taking a boat out on the reservoir on a nice day, catching a few white bass in eden.

we will invent a photosynthetic algae-symbiont, hybrid glass for high-rise windows. we will build the green spires of a future city, superhighways of the galaxy 3d-printed nests, 3d printed meat, artificial cherry flavor, self-replicating intersection system chain store migration, gas stations counting their neon numbers into the bright world, the bright world's work, proofs of concept, how to live, societal policing, beam me—outta here—Tyson chicken houses on the small highways, middle America, "above the fruited plain" Arkansas, their huge fans whirring in the heat—the stench—Go forth ye stunted dinosaurs—into the wilderness—stacked in filthy crates stacked and strapped down on flatbed trucks on the I-40, I-70, I-90 west, dirty white feathers floating, suspended for a second or forever above the hot asphalt in the shimmering air. 2,000 head of cattle died in Kansas last week from the heat. have you ever smelt a feedlot, heard the animal screams late into the night—what terror is—mammalian, lizard, deep and pure—mostly we keep these things hidden, in our country. we are human, after all, compassionate. the glossy interface, America—panopticon and aria of the new season—which is built on top the old season. they are growing pineapples in the glassed in dome of the Botanical Gardens in New York. the prisoners are leased out for unpaid labor. there are trees now growing on the arctic tundra. I saw that on the internet—bless the lemon seed, the indigo bunting, the cold soda in the glass case at the corner store, the mechanic who makes the car engine run, the spark plug, the faucet, the microscope, the microchip, the lithium mine, the fried-chicken sandwich, this is our one world, transformed—

massive beltways of the galaxy
thy rude materials

in hard ignorance and mammal dawn   awake
in obscenity and threaded soul   awake

remind your eyes   awake
excoriate your skin   like this

take me among   thy rude materials
lost—as always—in the shining   mucilage of my tiny self

world strands : black hole : gravity   lost   at the center of our galaxy
breathing, beating back   geometry of the known and unknown self

this soil: only one of many orifii   in starry heaven's vaulted vault
as mirror, eye and lake and worm   awake

snake eye, larvae of sleeping eons   in us   awake
grubs of a vast   and seamless empire

empty us   thy season of us

old lacewing   crack't bluejay egg; heaven's
hot asphalt's   fried hallelujah

these deep-buried gears will all   start turning soon
these are the spokes of the wheel   polished and gleaming

these are the spokes of the wheel   spinning outward
from your mind, your mind's eye   it is time.

I'm so glad you're here; you are just in time.   in my mind's eye,
image-strewn universe, engine of one eye, a thousand eyes
light-halo spokes out of the universe from a single point, radiant
breathtaking—

layer on layer, ganglion, dandelion, nebularized soul
lizard-eye, finch-eye, frog-eye, horse-eye, star-cluster
headlights, ignition coil, tuning-fork   wait
tune the heavens to us, breathe harder, deeper, wait
the sky is not an eye   it is the emptiness circling above us
as starlings turn   we will call it folding

it is not empty   it is the sheer film on our giant eye
through which   our gaze   graze   the haze
over the clearing   ozone, blink   smoke in the air column,
plume   one note played and then millennia of silence
all time gathers us up in its wide, callused hands,
pitches us into the data stream   just like that

we remember the palm of time's hand   time's infinite geometry
cheerful radiance of eons   crush us, grind us up

we are seeds in your bucket
we are grains about to get threshed
the bait—the hook—and the fish   all at once.

there is a light come down from somewhere
someday it will rain again

for example   there was once a beautiful world
for example, once   it rained for 200 million years

for example   we have no beaks, claws, or plumage, here
[but w thy mind, adorn these pistons of thought, grease them, turn them]

mascara; hands; wheels; lace : churned butter of the universe

until the green chrysalis forms, a white drop oozes at the tip
the red poppy opens   the great gears shift
the larvae wriggles in the dark   awake

forgive us : not   truant light-scape
stalk of a horny eden   heron-stalk   crab-eye stalk

spire-up-to-heaven-of-the-great-metropolis stalk   beam me
up, moss   first sensate fingers in the dark, awake

to make the measure of man, hominid, hominin, homonym, erect
to make man erect to the universe   awake

skymirror   satellites   break
International Space Station   break
North American Free Trade Agreement   break
the scaffolding that holds the bridge up   in our mind
the pistons, the fuel mixture, the 2-stroke oil
however it is that the internet   breaks
over all the minds gazing into the metaverse, continually breaks
like surf—like people running out into the crashing surf—

invent a fire making device
invent the wheel
invent the Air Conditioning Unit
invent a telescope and also a microscope
invent laughter
go look for your Very Own Soul Outward Then
in the now done glimmering darkness
where the worm of our soul sleeps dreaming
inventing its own glowing world-strands inside its larval world-self
the wildest dreams of the lucent larvae in the darkest dirt
as if it were any old Tuesday in the very last
topsoil of earth.

scissor-tailed flycatcher, alight over the electric vehicles
in the parking lot of heaven's state-owned park, the light
on the lake there, where you were in love, once

the honking of the geese hurt you then
do they hurt you now

nest making : ritual
if you can bear it

one big nest all together,
you probably can't bear it, poet

GREGORIAN MONKS SINGING THE HALO THEME SONG IN REAL TIME IN A REAL CHAPEL

Chilean copper mines: conduit   indicator of the future   plummet of Market Futures   yield on the 10-year T-note   which is a contract   which exists in our imagination   which is the first thing
NASA's yearly budget exists   so bless us harder

chrysanthemum-eyes of my dog in the sun   that incandescent nuclear-fusion gas ball hanging up above our heads   locked in the incomprehensible dance of our orbit   bountiful and merciless   the sun which holds the script of life's first desire for itself   on our planet   the sun which I would shoot out of the sky with a gun right now if I could   that evil god's blinding eye beating, bearing down—   scorching my tomatoes
the fragility of each thing   the resilience of all things   the specificity of care—

"why are the bees dying in the fields but thriving in colonies on the rooftops of Chicago?" the radio asks. bless the biologists and the beekeepers; bless the huge network; talk to me about a hypothesis, which is a hopefulness for the future—

the biologist on the radio says he is making a vaccine for bees   sometimes
I want to weep for people   all the people   doing all the things:
how on earth are you going to vaccinate the bees?

[by fields they meant suburbs—against a backdrop of lawns, the biodiversity of a city's habitat shimmers] the green lawns of America, sign, referent, symbol, signal symbiont of pesticide and fertilizer, green need, peace of the mower, ritual of tending, safe to lie down on: no stinging insects; no bees—

"to diversify your habitat to improve pollinator health," they say. things just, like, seethe. macro biodomic un-thought spread over the whole blue surface of this spinning blue ball   rocky mantle   magma core   plate tectonics of the writhing vibrant mining-sector insect-soul   claw and boom   eat some half-rotten thing, a piece of cheese, a pickled egg, mold will grow anywhere it's wet, invent a durable currency, gold or silver, copper, lead, beads, some glass, something beautiful you made, exchange something of equal value with a stranger and then go your separate ways, this is what freedom is, buy a lottery ticket, give a house-warming gift, a wedding gift, pass each other with a nod and smile, wave at the toddler in the cart, make a face, draw up a diagram, here are the plans for a house, for a city, here are the plans for an aqueduct, a skyscraper, a spaceship, here we go onward into the universe— listen to a story about bee scientists on the FM radio while sweeping with a broom you got from Walmart, it is now the 21st century since we started counting years this way, listen, almost as if to a prophecy to the dire warnings, predictions— "it's going to get bad real soon," my neighbor always says, and I say back "whatever, Jeff, people have been saying that *since the beginning of people*"— this, for us, is ritual. ritual motion around a center, ongoing tandem and two-step and pendulum of time. the sky, it is falling! later, the passionflowers are blooming over the beer cans in my trash pile, and I watch a gigantic bumble bee fumble, polite, around the center of flowering cucumber vine, covered in the yellow dust. it is a Sunday.

[now today] thunder and lightning all around but only a few drops of rain. I think I feel what my ancestors felt, what all our ancestors felt, a sort of deep and wild despair. I light a trash fire, part condemnation, part challenge, part prayer.

10-day weather forecast, bless
pollen count, bless, endless growth on a finite planet, bless

barcode [in what relation to] birdsong

we are lost somewhere in the collective imagination, aisles of fruit, magnetic ions in the upper atmosphere, factories that make toothpaste. "what price bananas," old greybeard; I'm with you in the aisles of active-wear, in the aisles of microwaves and frozen dinners, the wall of flat screen TVs revealing the many faceted face of god

doom-cube   doom-spiral
doom-vertical-plane   doom-cathedral
doom-greater-or-lesser-infinities   doom-mobius-strip
doom-aisles-of-humanity   doom-paradox-of-the-heap
doom-isles-of-humanity   doom-paradox-of-the-grain-of-millet
doom-parable-of-the-sower   doom-parable-of-the-choir
doom-paradox-of-the-faint-young-sun   the imaginary numbers
cluster in the dark around the darker   more imaginary center

leave the imaginary numbers alone! the calculus descends from the cloud to cover our shining bodies in its tiny increments. the doom leaks from the glowing portal between all hands, spread out, mucosal, grows, glows brighter and more merciful—like this we are holding hands all together. this is the optic nerve fiber of the world, looking back out at us. we blink in the formal logic, we kiss in the user-illusion, we undress in the particle-stream, we pick up a small stone and fling it at our own small horizon. try to break this whole thing open. the caterpillars are eating the leaves. the trees are sending out toxic alarm signals. the electric kettle is boiling in the quiet room. the oil refinery glows.

why not watch a relaxing 2-hour live squid cam from the Monterey Bay
Aquarium?   a YouTube time-lapse video of Pangea splitting apart   zoom
out to me standing in my kitchen dicing summer squash   sautéing its pale
green flesh in bacon fat and lemon juice   the James Webb Telescope
is taking pictures of the early universe   my dogs are asleep on the couch
covered in stars.   permission to be happy   permission to feel alive
permission to not be in pain   permission to let the dying things die
permission to not think about dying   permission to let the wine turn to
vinegar in the glass   the bread rises somewhere between the
yeasts and the singing

the morphology of the molting universe
all the prayers of the whole world, poured into a small cup

pour it out for us

the billions or trillions of yeasts and bacteria and viruses in a single cup
a single breath, a glass of rainwater, an inch of hair

a fly stuck in eden's net
a million flies a million webs
the photoreceptors in each fly's eye
like this the world kaleidoscopes outward and inward
folding, unfolding, calculating offerings

to calculate the trajectory of each atom in motion
would be to predict the entire future

no, say that there is chance built into the system
slight perturbations in an unstable equilibrium
as if it were a vast and seamless net flowing into time
as if we were fish returning to the rivers of our birth

hatchlings in the vast and seamless net, so weave—
we are hard wiring the universe outside of time
just for this one small moment on earth
a blip here, a blip there, blinking once or twice
folding over, maintaining this little
disequilibrium we call a household, a
body, a life

decay of an unstable orbit   caterpillars
are eating holes in the mainframe, fish
are spawning and dying in the rivers, don't worry,
this is how it has always been

this is the efficient flow-state of matter between time and time
this is where we will build the nuclear reactor
this is where the asteroid hit

don't worry, it is improbable you will fall through the electromagnetic
net of the atoms of the universe and come out the other side, awake—
unless…? the world will hold you. the world is holding you now.

accept the superconductors, reject the citrus
the price of a shipment of fish, you can grow
vanilla beans in Texas, I order rose harissa on eBay
$52 for a lot of 10 jars & "free shipping" from
the "United" "Kingdom," I order vanilla beans
from Madagascar, I spend all evening sitting
on a bucket with an aluminum beer can
on the ground next to me, connecting different pipe
and hose fittings to a small transfer pump, splitting
the existing water line with a brass barbed coupling,
moving between different pipe threadings, diameters,
affixing the black poly pipe with hose clamps, installing
air vents, splits, shunts, diversions and bypass lines.

it is all a project of planning, of forming the imaginary
system, drawing diagrams, thinking about air pressure,
gravitational pressure, fluid dynamics, what path water
might take inside the unseen, unknowable blackbox of
black tubing, laminar versus turbulent flow, of fitting forms
to their available components dumped out of the blue
Lowe's bucket onto the dirt ground in front of me, ultimately
to direct the world to my own more human ends
—this finite and particulate world inside the world—an acre
is what a person can plow in a day—in this case to direct the
available water from a distant spring into my catchment tank
so I can water my garden, take showers, do dishes.

the lead or copper pipes of each city sing through their geometric tangle
happily pumping the clear water up and up

wait, what—?

ritual motions of each level   the taste of sweetness or putrefaction
binocular vision   fiat currency   copper mines
city-zoning-commission-board   choices
corroded lead   zinc   flagella
how did we get here   how long it took us to get here

O nucleotide : shining rungs on the ladder; up. sugar & acid, up and up
O, twirl, you helix of abacus — round moon to the left over, yellow shell
station sign to the right, beads pressed between thumb and forefinger, seeds
or carapace crushed between teeth, concrete excrescence, our human histone
proteins same as yeast, the exoskeleton of my mind growing outward,
gnawing at the hard edges, the innumerable lineages, the symbiotic flow of
time, logging back into the network

first to conceive of, then to obliterate
heretic : of weeping [] small stones, hieratic,
an email from my mother, a quarter cup of rain
the Large Hadron Collider moans in the distance
the gulls fall from the cliffs and then glide out over an ocean
today, or one hundred
million years ago?
there is a stillness, and then there is the breaking

there is a stillness, and then there is the breaking.
impossible burgers, "meatless meat," 3d-printed eukaryote
of my same soul held in my same hands. there is the heat
and then there is the shadow, there is a certain pressure
in the air, we all share the weight of it, there is a relief
that will come after. I promise. I hope. there is somehow
a net amount of material on this here earth, just always shifting
between forms. "*or I may be a simple drop of rain,*
but I will remain…" "*and now it seems to me the beautiful*
uncut hair of graves" "and again and again and again" the rows
of sugar beets stacked in the fields, the smoke rising up,
graffiti on the overpass, how can we hold it all together?

upon closer inspection, the world is not, in fact, falling apart.

palindromic multiverse   shell-company   voiced syllabics sung out loud

one potato   two potato   three potato   four
what was once a root   caloric intake [of our] dominion
what was once a root   gigantic
and us with it   the shining monoculture fields of corn stand
irrigated in the desert   everything besides remains

we will build a high wall
we will build it out of stone
we will stack the stones in layers
we will build in windows
now we will make a marble column
now we will make a fountain of cool water
now we will make an arch
now we will charge a small coin for a lemonade
from our own citrus grove, where we grow
our lemons in the desert
now we will charge
a polarized battery cell with flow
of electrons from a circuit, clay vessel
there were rooms in Ephesus
in Dilmun and Aswan and giant
bones stacked on the tundra, cave
walls, that all the churches,
palaces, office buildings, apartments,
cement, steel, wood, glass and stone,
are excretions, mineral deposits, resource-
transfixed material out of this earth
out of this earth we live on top of and inside of
like little worms

in the high stone cliff : stone cities of the dead
one overlooking the ocean, one overlooking the river
the ocean necropolis and the river necropolis

we think even the dead might like to look out
of their stacked high stone honeycomb apartments
between the arched columns
from their dark expansive interiors
cut into the side of the mountain,
all together in the mornings.
like this memory is witness

like this memory is carved into rock
to hold the data of all the souls

like this memory is the braid that braids the past to the future
memory; the imagination of the past   cave, mind, myth or allegory,
a time   held out of time   held in the hands of our cathedral
carried forward   ancestors and ghosts   placed on our altar

memory is a bowl with a million holes
we pour it back and forth between us, sieve to sieve

memory is broken off fragments of the real
mutating, evolving, growing strange inside us
the mind is an ecosystem of divergent memories
coming together, coming apart, we roll
the universe down the hill together
and one by one we roll it back up

all writing is archeology

permission to 3d-print corals and put them back in the ocean. permission to surgically insert gps trackers into small fish, into eagles, into butterflies, into ourselves. permission to buy the Walmart eggs and the half and half of suffering. permission to go on loving someone. permission to pray for the death of a parent. what are we possessed by, today?

the threads, a tunnel in all directions. the meme on the internet says "you will experience the climate crisis as a series of videos on your phone until you are the one holding the camera." my sunflowers are 12 feet tall and bowing over with their own weight, the squash vines are 30 feet long and growing up trees, tendrils sprawling into the woods and across the driveway. a small rodent is eating my watermelons. I put out a live trap. the translucent shrimp in the plastic packaging, shipped up from the gulf, whole tiny lives, 20-30 to a package, the protein bonds, the complex eyes, whatever sentience is, whatever makes the refrigerator work. the sphere of the world as something between ritual and endurance. we are synchronizing the pulse in the deep mechanism, wheeling outward, this close to the whole expanse. there are new pictures of the universe on the internet today.

goldfinches on the mulberry tree   dirty windowpanes
shadow of finch and limb in parallel   third dimension, fight and flight
"Jackson, Mississippi to be without running water 'indefinitely'"

I put out birdbaths   the birds don't give a fuck
I watch a small vireo bathe like dancing in the puddle that drips from my AC
unit   the storm gathers in our heart   the sun is coming up
on the other side of that hill, there   the era of
filaments-in-lightbulbs   the era of the Ethernet-Cable
the era of swimming in the rivers   the sense of contamination
passed back and forth between us, on the internet   why
is everyone so far away   just there, right at my fingertips

a stone placed east and a stone placed west
like this the world is a vessel for memory

memory, which, briefly, biologically, exists, somehow
outside of time

the river is drying up   in Utah and Colorado   footprints of children playing in the mud   like all children   like all mud   city water pipes have to maintain a certain level of pressure exerted though the entire length of the system, pressing outward at the cracks, or else sewage, toxic chemicals, or whatever sludgy mire they run through might seep *in*
the forever chemicals cause cell mutation   the forever chemicals in the blissful rain   there is no next time in which we are more beautiful
more fuel efficient   have sharper more specialized beaks   a greater capacity for care

"before empathy became a cultural value," a book about the middle ages says

picking a few fruits in eden, picking a few seeds to save.

build grace into the technologic
interstice of the individual

relic of memory : reliquary

experience of the world : O in thy
one Geometry, many Geometries, speak
between us, each other, get me a purple soda, why don't you, excess
electrons joyriding around the superhighways of our mind, just
driving down a small highway in the Milky Way
again tonight

in the summer here the horse flies come out, giant, 1 cm diameter proboscis, hone in on us warm blooded aspects of their landscape, slow moving mountains to their time-stamped eyes. they are driving my dogs crazy, rain, finally, all things spring back, those that didn't die. that's how it goes. vascular structure of a cucumber vine, cellular geometrics in tree trunks suck up that water, baby, grow that crystal matrix, build those complex sugars, what is the structure of thought?

permission to buy lemons 4 for $3.00 permission to walk down bright aisles looking at bright objects, salad bowl, air-fryer, soft hoodies just in time for fall, permission to choose between scented and unscented trash bags, I throw the cold leftover french fries on the ground for my dogs when we get home in the dark.

NASA is uploading high resolution pictures of the Tarantula Nebula to flickr.com: there are auroras on Jupiter, there is liquid water on Enceladus, how long now since we became unbound from earth, germinate, Copernicus, we will show you how, we will save the best for last, whole galaxies rising behind the McDonald's drive-through window, behind the Exxon Mobile station, at the intersection of today and tomorrow, where yesterday just drove by, north to the football stadium, south to my holler, west to the lake, east to Memphis, and further, to the coast the windmills singing just off shore, sing to me, the gps-tracked whales. heat index of the future, entropy of the incandescent Now.

thresh : hold   cumulative [cumulonimbic] : what we don't know :
collective work builds the cloud   threshing and holding   at the edges   ants
bearing down on the universe   the hot engines of the universe turning in us
and isn't it here for us to see it   isn't it showing off   revving its beautiful
engine   vying   to be stroked gently by our instruments   dressed up
in its best   plumage   perfume   reeling at all the very edges of our soul
why don't you learn the new dances on the internet   juvenile humans love
to dance

"to see and be seen" in the interstitial miasma
anthropomorphizing ourselves in the checkout line

frying fish in the fry baskets of the universe
weird grapes : weird wine
weird human minds [] human tools
inverse relation: longing : longing
time's seeds germinate at night
as a water drop : reflects

I fill up each day as if I am filling up a cup, as if
I am rolling a small rock up a small hill.
time is a material I move through

hack out a piece of it
supersaturate, a gift—

accretion : acceleration [disc] [dilation]
conception of the many spheres, dial-up,
era of ozone layer, era of Hormone Replacement Therapy,
era of synthetic oil for high milage engines for $34.99, era of digital data,
era of emailing your mother YouTube videos of baby animals, would you
upload your consciousness to a distributed processing cloud if you could
would you inject nano-robots into your bloodstream
to edit your genes to not suffer, genetic anomaly
of the data stream, heart defect, throat cancer, fibroids in the transcriptase.
we still die in this era of infinite horizons, flickering lights, specialize
me, instruments, at every level, fractal of endless coastlines,
calculus of sand grains, human-sized feet, limbs, human-sized lives
lived out in the speeding superhighway of time, human-sized deaths
all go down the wide watershed of the Mississippi forever

116°F in Sacramento yesterday, the radio says, the state is asking, via text
message alert, for people to voluntarily reduce their electricity usage to avoid
rolling blackouts in the power grid, okay, shared world, can we
handle it? or will it break us, just now, when we are
so close?

the smell of fire on the air, the pink sky   one sign of sentient
alien life, astronomers say, could be tell-tale traces of energy production:
pollution in the atmosphere of other planets, like ours.

three perfect romaine hearts raised in the fields opposite of mercy
three perfect romaine hearts a light emerald green wrapped in clear plastic
three perfect romaine hearts for $4.99 in the temperature-controlled aisles of
paradise salt and mayonnaise and soft pajamas in the aisles of paradise

"the relationship between the Federal Reserve and the World," the radio
says, "poached eggs in a harissa tomato sauce," the website says…
Arendt says that Democritus said "a victory of the mind
over the senses could end only in the mind's defeat" a victory…
of the mind… over the senses… could only end… in the mind's…
defeat? around and around, we go…

cuneiform: a logo-syllabic writing system
the press of the style into soft clay, the notation, the baking,

the intent to preserve a thing in a durable memory
lossless .wav file, compact disc, MP3, Blu-ray, thumb-
drive, double helix, golden disc. reentrant signaling at every level,
at every edge of every world, loop. I want to lie down outside
but there are too many bugs

rhesus monkey of my soul, yellow-breasted bowerbird of my heart, blue-tailed skink of my optic nerve, great blue whale of my veins, tiny golden beetles of my consciousness crawling about on the surface of everything all around me, eating holes in the green leaves, laying metallic eggs, mutating in the blazing light.

which is the error and which is the code
error : code : daisy, make me a chain there
chimera in the celestial mechanics

the wine of forgetting is also the wine of remembering
here's to the wine of forgetting and also to the wine of remembering

like this memory fills a vessel
the shape of its own shape outside of time

DUNG BEETLES NAVIGATE BY THE
MILKY WAY the spaceweather.com news email reads

to separate the molecules of the one drop
of water you once poured into the sea

unpour one out for us
here is my cup

the volatility of the markets, the humpbacks singing in the sea
blue is the color of my heart, ventricle and atrium of tides

the frivolous prayers set down next to the broken drive-chain of the universe
wedding vows next to axle shaft, kinship rituals, timing belts, death rites
whole ecosystems of love, violence, oxytocin, belonging, socket sets, gesture,
scent signal, mechanism, grief, constraint

promise [in some relation to] future, Arendt suggests. "durability," Arendt writes. butter churned in huge vats in the aggregate facilities of the universe, which is itself the promise of a future. milk from the billion domesticated cows of the universe, what love is, stored in stainless steel silos of the universe, for your morning coffee, ritual and pleasure, where is the pasture? how far. how green is your pasture, today? the grazing animals graze, they have evolved two stomachs, four stomachs, for fermenting the hard fibers and harder seeds of the open fields of our small planet turning us over gently in the sun, like an egg.

what is the aggregate data of every sensation on earth,
the amalgam of a composite mind, which is history itself
lying awake on the surface of the world, tossing and turning
restlessly across the surface of the world?

archiving eden: the doomsday vault
sheer off the melting: cliff ice our blue heart might
bloom another day, bindweed, morning glory, choke weed
planting in red clay: consider putting a pasture there instead
where we live and how we live, electric wizard and mined lithium
batteries and solar array. next we will 3d-print the meat, the wheat,
the knee-joints, the photo-reflective camera lens on the space station
sailing outward, the next years next horizon, thus we will be in the image of,
the water-melon seeds will grow in your stomach if you swallow them, they
will grow up their electric green vines out of your pink and choking throat,
they will grow vibrantly into the bright sunlight of the unreal world around
us, more real than any words in any language yet invented
by men or beast, by men or beast of soil, toil or well-oiled soul.

"the US isn't going to grow a semiconductor industry overnight," the radio says. "uninhabitable" I write. Ava tells me she used to think it was better to eat one big animal than many small animals, a 16 oz bag of shrimp, like 30-40 souls. better to eat one whole cow. in the Ozarks we have "disappearing creeks" a function of the Karstic geology, the creek goes below the level of its topmost stones and below the water keeps flowing, full of crawfish and small minnows. the creek rocks are dry though, up here, they are steadily growing brighter, white stones, dry bones, blinding calcified exoskeletal excreta of our ancestors, crown of ghost-crabs scuttling across the deep ocean floor of our ancient mind. they say it will be another couple of years before our semi-conductor industry is really thriving. spiders were the first out of the sea, they can hear through the external-mind technology of their satellite-dish-shaped web.

cruciform & treacherous kiss; skies; leap, spoil, soil; wheat, rice, seed-grass all the same; *poaceae,* barley, oats, wheat, rice, corn, rye, all grass, just grass, monocot of that first spring, first flat molars to grind the hard grain; roll down from heaven the baleful sheaves, then roll them back up with your knobby knees, like this memory is an act of gathering, like this memory grinds us

like this memory gathers itself up into mountains, mounds, composites, what relation of recorded history [to] history's record. winnow, hands, wear down, time—Appalachian Mountains older than the dinosaurs, cryogenic vault of magnetic earth spreading out beneath us, data-crunching the rocks under us. the steady transformation, roll down from the heavens the joyful electrons. the compressor kicks on in the dark, the magnets spin around a center—

it will take voyager one thirty thousand years to fly through the Oort Cloud, that ice-gravel cell-membrane of our solar system, blink. (the sleep is in your eyes)

there is the sound of people laughing, sailing off into the dark reaches
someone will find it long after we are gone. I would bet on it.

"is cloud-seeding stealing another country's water," the radio asks?
here we are, in the future.

what is owed, what allotment
to whom, what allotment is owed in this life

in this life or any other on this earth,
on this earth or any other?

the da **da** da **da** da **da** da **da** : the awe and awful order, leaking gasket ruinous and ecclesiastical. there is voltage at the power stations, there is nerve circuitry that drives the hard-eyed people you see walking by, on a Wednesday, small shoulder of small highway into town, addiction center, bus stop, Mr. Taco Loco, a world emptied of people is a wilderness, a world emptied of kinship is a wilderness, asphalt jungle for whom the State is the only safety net, in times of peace, we can build a garden. what is bountiful? what is multiply? as soon as conditions are right, the yeasts divide. if you have enough, if you have hands. we have to do our work to maintain the myth, each of us, weave its tendrils across the bridge of time, infloresce, connect us each to each. the network clicks on, hums, blinks back at us. there is nothing to comprehend, this unending, unfolding Rubik's Cube and mirror of our collective soul. the network's algorithm shows me people dancing, shows me how to cook a fish, shows me 7 habits of mentally healthy people. take me to your leader. I have to admit a certain fear, something about ants, apes, and death, and vastness, something about a capacity for care.

we are surrounded by a shell-of-signals flying outward, Frank Drake of the Drake Equation says on the radio, a segment from before he died. "anyone who is looking will know we are here," he says, "we don't have to advertise." what caused 49 Starlink satellites to fall out of orbit, the headline reads. a geomagnetic storm caused by a solar flare, the article answers. like this memory is a shell of detritus in, on, and around us. like this memory is a question and an answer. we are our own archipelago of wreckage. like this memory is an active archeology. the sentience is in the hands.

entropy in what relation to the broken cup
[] as it is breaking…

like this it is breaking : the light come up in shafts, "the day," we say, "it breaks," we say, splits shadow from form, limb from finch, wake up, the shadows move, the day is long, we have to get going, there are things to do, we have to calculate some trifecta of prayer, circumference, need. the obelisk, the sundial, the sense of the globe spinning, as if we were a fixed point, as if we could fix some point, with a wrench or socket set, get this thing spinning again—

permission to go inside, away from all the insects. permission to be somewhere quiet, just to think. the end of the world, as in the inner end of a telescope through which everything looks tiny and far away. someplace out of all this wind and fast-vast-flowing time.

I drive toward an eastern star, falling forward. 1037 mph, give or take my current speed. driving east means you are falling faster.

fractions of prayer, monuments of prayer, domesticated thistle of prayer, conundrum of levers by which we heaved up off the world, scaffolding and architecture of prayer, the self-check-out register beeps, a speaker speaks from overhead: "please step forward to register twenty-three." "we are all in this together." "please scan your items, then place them in your bag." the hand held laser scanner scans the white space in the barcode, like this meaning is encoded in the spaces between things, meaning rings up my lettuce, lemons, beer. "and I say to myself..." comes on over all the loudspeakers of heaven. "what a wonderful..." I walk alone in the aisles of paradise, out the automatic sliding doors and into the piped in music and majestic sunsets of America's parking lot.

"the inverted-yield curve" okay, Catabasian,
I will show you what the inverted yield curve does,
it yields. but will it yield...to you? what slimy thing is climbing up
sentience's next steep graph out of the ocean, trough and crest and surge with
what love out of the carbon fields, the glittering numbers into the upper
atmosphere, dancing like the hem of the mad god's garment, bluer than blue,
more ochre than hands, this magnificent new rift
opening inside us

Galileo made a flipbook of the sun; it showed that it was spinning.

to calculate the RPMs of earth the sliced-time dichotomy
parse parsec & idling engine haze of insects lift up off the bluestem
prairie grass that naturalized here go back
uncrack the egg start today over you've already
messed this one up NASA hit an asteroid
with a small spacecraft, yesterday, 11 million kilometers away

Marc writes to say that the RPMs of earth is 24 hours divided by the earth's circumference. I type "24 / 40,075" into google and get "The Catechism of the Catholic Church in Question and Answer Form" what

"in thee hell"?

"Neither asteroid poses a threat"

"stupid little planet full of monkeys" we will come out
swinging our hands full of ripening fruits
probably grinning the world is too big and the earth is too small,
a childhood in the metaverse on earth as it was in heaven
on earth as it was in SimCity on earth as it is in Tetris
a childhood in the goldilocks hypothesis a childhood bored in the simulation

the article says, "maybe the metaverse that we get
is the metaverse we deserve" (derogatory)

as fear relates to prayer hold in one hand a small rock
in the other the whole history of the universe which is heavier
pitch them both as far as you can, azure vault 'n all feeble arc 'n all
"towards justice" 'n all "rage, rage" 'n all pick up your things, honey,
it is time to go.

the sun waits for no man. it is a burning ball of gas.
what could it know of waiting. it will go out someday.

google-fact-checking your poem:
"our star will grow to be larger than we can imagine"

to talk with your friends about love, about heartbreak, "the hurricane," he said, "raged all night, at least the house was still standing." it is just the things that life is made out of. where does it hurt today, on a scale of 1 to 10, on a scale of 1 to want-to-fling-yourself-off-a-cliff. "perhaps the birds will feel the expanded air with more passionate flying." it is like someone is pouring time between our fingers, our cupped hands; everything flows out through the net of time. Elise, I forbid you to be in pain, I forbid anyone from hurting you. I will make the world stop spinning. I will cut heaven in half and hold out the bigger half to you, dripping in the sunlight, in the parking lot, the sticky pink juice of a flayed and skewered heaven, the flies, the yellowjackets, the pollinator wasps, the yeasts already converting the sugars; it will be a celebration.

I walk alone in the aisles of paradise

we walk together in the aisles of paradise

I'm with you in the aisles of paradise, buying socks

WHAT IS THE MYSTERIOUS "GLOBAL HUM"–AND IS IT SIMPLY NOISE POLLUTION?

are you ready to get MAD? are you ready to get MADE IN THE IMAGE OF? are you ready to refinance your mortgage? have you chosen the right necropolis? upload your consciousness to heaven's gigantic supercomputers! please step forward to the next available register! scan your items against the names pre-written in the book of heaven, in the symbolic writing of the barcode language of the vaster sentience! Everything is on Sale! Everything Must Go! okay. I am going. I am going now. this is my last will and testament; cut the concertina wire; force glucose into the electric grid; burn all the prisons; get someone to take care of my mother, Houston, we have taken on a new form—there was a problem—it laid itself out before us—inviting—we always rise to the occasion—we are in love with the problem—we have chosen to follow the problem down all the small highways of America, stopping for gas station coffee and a cold hard-boiled egg wrapped in plastic and genetically identical apples while the wavelengths of sound pipe in over the gas station radio and leak into the night. "I'm carrying your love with me / West Virginia down to Tennessee." I will find a new dimension, a better one. "sorry you have missed us. if it is urgent, text URGENT, if not, please leave a message after the tone."

[and then there was 2 billion years of the sound of rocks grinding]

THIS IS ONLY A TEST   THIS IS A TEST OF THE CITY'S EMERGENCY WARNING SYSTEM   THIS IS ONLY A TEST

"it's like you always come to town on a Tuesday." I am lying in the sun with our three dogs and Marc is standing over me, taking a picture of us

like this memory needs tending, us notching off days
on the long femur of time, days which are just rotations
into and out of the field of the sun

solar system; metronome
binomial pulse % heartbeat of []

permission to eat the rotisserie chicken of suffering
in the truck in the parking lot while the sun sets, permission
to acknowledge the despair gnawing at the edges, permission
to close our eyes, just for an instant, to see the galactic
static waiting there.

> *when I get home I water my garden in the dark, Sagittarius drawing his bow at the crescent moon in front of me, Cassiopeia at my back: do you know what way I'm facing? I am facing away from earth, holding a rubber snake of water, trying to hold a circumference in my mind, in my mind's eye opening outward. to tend what needs tending is a constant practice.*

"use it or lose it," the physical therapist says. I think of electricity sparking short between neurons, a signal with nowhere to go.

the radio says the biomass of all the ants on earth is roughly equal to the biomass of all human beings on earth. I picture ants coalesced in the shape of a human. I picture all humans on earth made of ants, going about their daily human business, all chemical signals and motion. I am squeamish before the awe & squeamish at the interstice, squeamish at the intersection where the cars and trucks stop and go. we evolved these colors to see the fruits, red in the green branches, stop, green in the cathedral array, go. what is your rubric for intelligence, roseate of highway loop and curled geometries clicking in our one eye, lights flashing in the other, silverfish flash in the shallow water, electric pulsing outward? this is the long procession of souls, souls stuck in traffic, stuck in the cuneiform logic, stuck on the transversal plane on the highways of myth—Los Angeles, St. Louis, Nacogdoches, Silver Dollar City, Broken Arrow, Greenville, Waukegan, Rio Grande, Manhattan—helicopters whirring overhead.

I don't know how many days it has been since it rained. cracks are opening up in the earth, in the hard dirt, in the garden, in the driveway. I worry if it rains the cracks will fill and cleave this place apart. the creek is dry as bones bleached in the brute southern sun, bones strewn in hot moonlight. it is a full moon tonight.

there is a sense in which the earth itself is our shared technology

Dallin said a man on TV said if you erased the history of all the religions and all the gods and all the myths right now, in 10,000 years you would have all new myths, new gods, new religions, but if you erased all of scientific knowledge right now, in 10,000 years we would have rediscovered mostly the same knowledge, give or take some spurs of interest in different directions. to grow a real or imaginary net, to grow a real and imaginary net over the world that must be here underneath it all, somewhere, touch it gently, prod it forward, watch it move across the surface.   squeeze out the vesicle and draw a pattern on the wall, watch the ants flow along it, touching antennae as they pass on the ant superhighway, you can even write your name, the name of god, a mathematical equation, draw a cock-and-balls. up above the satellites blink. what on earth are they doing down there, they think.

they say they don't know why the earth's rotation is slowing down.

if the moon is full the sun is behind you.

> in *The Internet Is Not What You Think It Is: A History, A Philosophy, A Warning* Justin E. H. Smith writes in a chapter called "The Ecology of the Internet": "why should we not see our own technology as natural technique? [...]
>
> prairie dogs calling out to their kid...
> sagebrushes emitting airborne methyl
> jasmonate to warn others of their kind...
> blue whales singing songs for their own

inscrutable reasons, perhaps simply for
the joy of free and directionless discourse
of the sort that human beings
call by the name of chatting."

"like the fact that they can see through my body and through her body into the roof of her mouth is so wild" and "it's so wild that she has a full skeleton" Elaine texts about her baby growing inside her. "the tech-heavy Nasdaq tumbled," "*Earth: Final Conflict* season 5 is coming to streaming," the plants suck carbon out of the air to build their rigid cells, bend toward sunlight. the competition for sunlight that made all these elongated trees towering over each other, totally ridiculous. weight-load tells your bones where to grow denser, you architectural city, you.

the pork sector
the poultry sector
the humane stun-guns of the 21st century, bless
they restarted a dead pig's brain with chemicals, bless

Candy Crush, FarmVille, Call of Duty, Forge of Empires, bless
that the world's awaiting us   googling its own soul in the infinite, bless

vast and vacant   inanimate canopy   digital leaf   digital fat   digital sorrow
digital optic nerve   gut microbiome   make decisions for me   panopticon
and outer space   net amt of species in a wetland prairie   in a city block   in
the 4 stomachs of a hoofed ungulate   in your belly-button umbilicus hole
the membranous zone between eyeball and eye   secrete a recursive
loop   and live inside it   believe me   I don't know anything—
except how to live inside a recursive loop—

or maybe this is all the video-game simulation of some lesser god

finally, today, this morning, hail.
thunder, lightning, smaller spire off the
main storm, air heavy, ancestral, didn't
get the wood in, don't care, dogs asleep
on the couch, the bird trembling as if she
forgot about thunder even though she's
been five years on this planet. I text Ava
"I almsot cried"

they are transplanting human brain cell clusters into the brains of rats, the radio says. the transubstantiation of animal souls, perceptive apparatus of each species. I take a picture with my phone of a dragonfly, nature's top predator, 90% kill rate, compare to a lion, 25%, on my fake-silk curtain, those crazy eyes, how does it see me, the lens of my phone looming over it. "you might also be interested in *which animal or insect kills its prey in the most horrifying manner?"* the website suggests. I just might.

the meme reads : [guy inventing an arrow] "I'd stab that guy if I wasn't so far away" like this human technology elides time and collapses space : like this the artifact is the memory and notation of that collapse : the stitch in the fabric over and under us. the stitch that stitches us to us, to each other, to time, to the world.

"It's hard to make out" the
article reads "but [the scientist]
tells me that I should be able
to see a mostly clear, light film
on the bottom of the vial—this
is the DNA. But this DNA is
special. It does not store the
code from a human genome,
nor does it come from any
animal or virus. Instead, it
stores a digital representation
of a museum.

in San Diego there are miniature human brains growing in petri dishes producing coordinated waves of electrical activity. the article says they terminated the experiment "to avoid the creation of consciousness." OK. let's try to a v o I d t h e c r e a t I o n o f c o n s I o u s n e s s .... the computer autocorrects a singular "i" to a capital "I"—automatically generated selfhood in the worldhood of the inter-face. okay. face me. interesting. my senses mine me, electric gems, nerve of electric ore, body half gore half glory, what is it that animates the eye, the blink and flinch, bloom iris then contract, come crash up upon these rocky spires, these digitized shores. "oh my god" and "here we are".

"Physicians generally assess the level of consciousness in patients in a vegetative state on the basis of whether the person blinks or flinches in response to pain."

so flinch in response to pain, to show 'em you're alive.

whether or not the "internet" is "empty"
whether or not the "universe" is "real"

"the milky way" "the silver river" "the backbone of night"
"the route of scattered straw" "the great fence of the stars"
"the reflected path"

the space between atoms. that it is mostly void. lightning between the membrane and the pasture. and between, the turbulent flow, the bandwidth of all life

my mother emails me that they have taught brain cells to play the old computer game "Pong" in which a ball bounces back and forth across a void.

"rock on" is how my mother signs her emails

[] sky-train to concourse C
they are selling sun-chips
they are partnering with breast cancer

it is still a quilted-grid patchwork of 40 acre
multiples and combine radii square root of green electric-
cell bacterial cluster and node, from above: mostly still,
mostly still empty, mostly flat except these places where time
gathered up her rocky hem. we fly west

at sunset. and then it is a river of light, moon-
glint running along the silver rails, pile
of burning coals, stretched
along the grid-oaths, flow of energy
within the systems, Krebs-cycle of a
land-locked mid-sized American city at dusk
glittering necklace, star and mine field, rib-
osomal accretions backlit and blinking, pass those
electrons back and forth with me, quarries
for and of the hearts of men.

then east. 747 jumbo jet over the huge dark lung-shaped lakes
we sit in rows, each glowing orb a screen
20,000 feet above the earth, something of comfort,
something of stupor, something of wonder.
they are coming down the aisle with beverages ginger
ale coke sprite alcohol available for purchase for pleasure.
cranberries are real fruits; they exist they grow
in salt-marsh bogs in the actual world "and yet
a bit of the true self exists..."

now south. by train past highway auto salvage chevy blazer ford
Econoline 350 Subaru Hyundai Elantra hoods up exposed
engines full of blown down leaves mud puddle metal
carcass crumpled wheels stacked over green duckweed river
in leaf light all yellow and constraint. a man in a reflective vest
sumac sumac solar panels in a lot gives way to motorboats
lawns two and then three-story houses. time putrescent
chipping away its layers manifesting its ordered accretions its

dividends sugars fleeing the leaves in that final flame-fire of emptiness
carbon and soul sucked back down to soil…

the wide Housatonic or maybe it's the Connecticut Allegheny
or the Delaware I don't care so far north the sun is angled here
comes in across all things weak and cold but blazing
gold if I will admit it. (I will admit it) (I hate it here)
double propeller helicopter over river.
train tracks, an hour late, red leaves dipping into
their own reflection phragmites, invasive golden sheaf
reflected up and down, a heron. graffiti under the overpass
and the overpass over the overpass and all the monstrous trees.

the monstrous trees all dangling
excrescence ragged cellular miasma
just hanging in the wind extruding bits of themselves
into this dimension as parts tendrils as badly copied
repetitions leaf and leaf fragments breaking off from the impossibility
and inevitability of a whole scattering lending
their molecular architecture to a climbing other. what is it
that is growing here? what is reflected out of that green mire? materia
and muck in the long prism, turning now yellow now scarlet now fall.

who knows what will happen to America's decrepit old cities, brute and empty rows and rows, worn-thin, wore-out century, brutal architecture, cubes and curved concrete, worn-down curbs, trash blowing along the dingy multiverse, the America we deserve, decrepit old Dunkin' Donuts, Radioshack artifact, C&C tune 'n lube, empty box stores, bars on the windows, stray dog of stray joy, a wind picks up, the streets are ghosts, the dead shall rise again the archway says, different dimensions folded in the world, the banal physicality of a still barely inhabitable earth, what we have lost, still earth, earth still earth, dirty and hot, O no the ornate archway's parabolas are closing in.

now I'm stuck in the dimensional collective geometry of human imagination, as snails make whorled and spired shells, we build our cities, this videogame, virtual-reality graphic universe has no exit. this grass, so green; this marble, so white; the archways marching in the inverse mirror, forever. here you are, nothing can hurt you here. the DNA of cities in the crystal matrix, beetle larvae are chewing through the layers of time.

what on earth are we going to do with all these people? they are lying on the grass, they are laughing, they are eating snacks. further out from the center, bulldozer parked in a dirt field, scrap metal, spindly new growth briars over old railroad ties, America, build dry-wall smart homes with talking refrigerators chock-full of "the future" super-food energy-drinks, LED lights at 100hz. three men sit on a park bench in sunlight near a bare-limbed tree surrounded by its own scattered circle of red, delinquent alley, rusted freight container, "wish you were here / from the other side, billy," "STD-gang," whole lives lived out in traffic, as if the colors were enough to live on. the colors are not enough, not enough to calm this violent flight response in me. I am helpless and carried along, the conductor comes for my ticket.

LaGuardia sky walkway to terminal G in slant beams of light, I watch stuck traffic over the overpass and think of Odysseus, then a great blue heron in the muck estuary beyond the concertina wire and dirty highway trying to eat a fish that's too big for it, or maybe it's dead, or a sock covered in mud. I watch as I wait to be called. "first it will be platinum," she says, "then gold, followed by diamond, then comfort plus, then comfort, then sky," she says. the Archimedean point, trifecta and grid and wind-scattered light, each to each, she says. “have a good day!” she says.

Time, she says
will tell,

she says, the story
of ourselves

this spinning blue green gold computer chip mother board
round as a spent blessing in the minefield of space

days are flowers around their suns in the field of spaces endless night
they are turning their many-petalled faces, hydrogen, helium, oxygen,

nitrogen, carbon-based, vibrating electrons, turn the light
on my love, make coffee, let's get this thing

straightened out between us. one life and on either side of it
eons and eons of nothingness stretching

out for ever. you have to plow the right field
in the muon-rain and pirouetting quarks, you have to tend

the right pasture. we didn't build the world, but
it forms the shapes that shape our life, time, trajectories and us.

time, my friend, is *of the essence*, we are for-the-time beings
and the globe is spinning beneath us. we are time-beings, metabolizing
the now into the past, behind us, sending out its glowing strands behind us.

calf canyon ; hermit's peak ; wingspan of my country
Sangre de Christo ;
storm moving in from the west O wide swath O durational motion

rising smoke from wildfires seeds, thunderstorms as the ash
and soot rises in the currents of upper atmosphere, bless

"marking one's territory" "to leave a mark" "to tell a story"—which is a project of memory "I Ozymandais was here" have left this trace here, this scent, this monument, piss-mark, obelisk, prayer-flag, trash-heap, satellite, or ode : "Cody was here 2022" carved into *this* stone the world will say, *this* acre, for a little while, before the killing frost, when the rains came, what it asks of us, mammal body, mammal kin-recognition, mammal seeking, we will scratch our names in any rock, the bark of any tree, scrawl it in bar and gas station bathrooms "here" is an archive of presence, so-and-so on this date in time, the living memory shapes the world, gathers sticks for the digital nests, world-strand, electric heater, honeycomb cities with their clanking pipes "humans were here," they will say, inscribed on the surface, grown over, crushed under, heaved up, after

"Herodotus" or "Keeping Up with the Kardashians" all the same
Twitter into the void all the same

it is raining in a wide east-moving band from Duluth all the way down
to Dallas all the same

the sugars go down from the leaves, permission to try again, permission to bake the blue cake, to cover the blue cake in edible glitter I got from the internet, permission to fill the eyeball piñata with liquor, weed gummies and skittles, permission to do our best, to throw horseshoes, to blindfold Jeff even though he's drunk, spin him around, laughing, let him take a swing at the thing, ritual of repeated motion braiding its braid of meaning through time, "99 apples" somehow in one tiny, horrible bottle, "there is a pear tree between here and West Fork," I say, "the west fork of the White River, we should go get them soon, maybe make some cider"

permission to try again, press some sugars out of the damned materia

pear trees take a long time to grow; the saying is "you plant pears for your heirs"   like this memory can be a gift: a sort of hopefulness that there might be a future,   someone to enjoy it

"we can let some go to vinegar," I say,   "and what we don't drink as cider
we can run through the janky ebay still"   pear-persimmon moonshine ;
"and yet a trace of the old self exists…"   transubstantiation of sugars
into the future sorrows or joys all the same   most animals don't have
sugar receptors   some insects taste with their feet
what is sorrow to an insect

it's good to remember to fuck before the party, oxytocin-hack for feeling sweet in the midst of all the people.

the moon's rose madder in composite image : capture
photons from the upper atmosphere, gather all the images
together, come, fovea and nerve cell and ganglion,
fold over on yourself, awake. it will be a celebration

"worldmaking is a territorializing process" someone posts on the internet.
"deep down in the bible-black vents" writes Nick Lane in his book about the
biochemical origins of metabolic processes

I am trying to tell you something about the architecture of time
I am trying to understand something about the structure of the shared universe

I am trying to build a nest, in our minds, together
out of everything, all together. as if we could bear that, poet.

that it is a universe to all but a multiverse to each
or the opposite, I don't know, vice versa? I have to go

sweep my small corner of the universe; the dogs track in
so much dirt; I have to make breakfast, two or three eggs on toast.

the shining fats, the protein strands, the sugars, the yeasts, the sun
streaming in at an angle now, the music of the spheres is getting louder—

the sound of a distant chainsaw, laughter, maybe where you are,
traffic or birds or construction or wind down the canyons of avenues

honking horns, sirens, a TV in the next room, the sound
of someone cooking, someone playing an instrument, vibrations

in the molecules of air, the radio playing Bach or Megan Thee Stallion
or marketplace morning report

isn't there some oscillating connection between a cycle and a trajectory?
this is the calendar of the future, sailing outward, this is how a battery works

one question in the search
for alien life is the relatively
small window of geologic
time between the discovery of
burning carbon as an energy
source and environmental
collapse, a quickly resolved
instability over the eons
of change on a planet, a
blip barely recorded in the
stratosphere, faint line of ash,
era of high CO2 affecting
pollen sugar density for a
while. the question is the
statistical likelihood of the
co-incidence of our slim
window of consciousness +
technological advancement
into space exploration, and
theirs.

whole civilizations blooming
and going out on planets all
scattered in the darkness—one
by one the lights come on and
one by one the lights go out—

all cycles are rituals
your tracking number will be provided

think of every chicken egg on earth, right now, palm-sized
fruit or cell or orbit. there is a way

the present can cannibalize the future,
the Pleiades come up in the powerline cut, now

my mother emails me "my credit cards
aren't working, please bake me a cake

with a metal file in it" and
"the hawks are migrating, again!"

ants are a game played by chemicals
humans are a game played by myth

supply-chain disruptions "uncoiled"
humans are a game played by markets

Caterpillar tractor, Texas Instruments, Boeing signed a deal for
8,000 more machinists and aerospace engineers. the GDP

contracted again. this rocky birth, weird chrysalis, phase-converter, please
algorithm, know which podcast to autoplay next, "nearer

my god to thee…"

"weaker global activity…" "lowered demand for grapes"
"what the actual price of raisins is right now in Tokyo" "speaking
of apples" "to dust we shall return"

sunlight and sugar : atoms and the void
dimensional time : to live inside

for thine is the kingdom, the phyla, the glory
for thine is the order, the genius, the species

don't mess this thing up for us, us apes of kinship and grief
at the corner of online shopping and heaven

at the corner of the combustion engine and All-Life-On-Earth
under this wide swath of infinitely expanding universe, bless

hungover in the place that synchs
my two eyes up into one World, bless

humans are not the only animal to partake
in what the yeast does to the grape, bless

all the monkeys that came before, bless
the fermenting sugars of my soul, all

eyeball and permission; yield, fruit; yield, world
the fermenting sugars burrowing into the soil, re-crystallize

chrysalis, matrix
come, it will be a celebration.

grace in the interstice of being, we will call it
another-year-of-being-alive, we will choose to call it a blessing

did you get drunk and leave your phone at Jeff's?
yes. no way to go but forward in time. nowhere to go
but up.

New Babel, New Uruk, New Arkadelphia, New Gate-
of-All-Nations, New Moon-Landing, New Rain-on-Genetically-
Modified-Wheat, New Blessings, New Cyanobacteria-Crusting-on-the-
Small-Rocks, small crustaceans exploring the chromatic topography of our
Mind, let us go out and
ask of it, the World.

let us go out and ask of it, the world which is hard and made of a hard
materia, electron-repulsion of negatively charged particles which is all you

have ever touched, neck, body of a lover, table, rock, the space between where atoms sing to the void, soprano, acapella, queen-of-the-night, king-of-the-road, master-of-puppets, come back to me, world, work of our hands

someone wrote me asking me to be in an anti-work anthology

who built your city, poured the concrete, asphalt, mined the silica, mined steel for the rebar beams, strung the wires the bright light flows through, where does pigment for paint come from? I don't know but what matters is someone knows, someone gathers it, someone mixes it, someone pours it in equally sized containers, someone drives it stacked in 18-wheelers across the highways of America, someone planted those trees or cut the old trees, sawmills cut that lumber, someone made that pizza, harvested that rice, the green rows, almost endless, ethanol-sunflowers, the hot engines quietly hum in the subway tunnels every 7 or 15 minutes, someone monitors the pressure valves that monitor the pressure over the tunnels so they don't collapse under the weight of the world we've erected that you walk on every day, grates you step over, the bridges will last longest after we are gone, architects and engineers of our collective soul, of our collective future, each copper pipe fitted all the way from the reservoir, where they built the dam and where they now build fish wheels to let the fish swim back up past the dam.

I'm not saying what's good for us is good for the planet, only that we build the world for each other, no human is alone, no human has ever been alone, goldilocks hypothesis of indoor plumbing, HVAC systems, inner sanctum built by other humans piece by piece, movie theatre, logarithm, electrocardiogram, open-heart surgery, solar battery, packaged meat, ibuprofen, the children will inherit only the world we give them, almost every single thing we encounter has been touched by human hands, fabricated, machined, shipped, rained on, mined, harvested, formed, homo faber, built and sapient world—

go lie down in a field and get eaten by bugs, see if I care

a better question is what we owe to the continuous lineage of that work

Annie from Little Rock and the Internet writes me, "they don't understand that energy is only free when it warms you in the sun. everything after that is entropic, forced movement."

the only planet we've got, they say:
inhospitable wet rock hurtling through a vacuum, okay.

built a warm kitchen in it, Alexa play
some sort of goofy fugue for us

for me and you, together

you have my permission to be a human being, we will renew your
subscription to the world, automatically, each day

unless you text STOP to 1-800-WHY AM I SAD TODAY
would you like to upload your consciousness to the Cloud?

to look down a microscope at
the molecular scripture of your soul? descent

of man, divergent of jellyfish, unhumble of abode, wet brained and hairless
of ape, imaginary friend of many deities, the mechanism

is always there, waiting to be discovered. call this faith
in our ability to understand the world we have just now

found ourselves in. ancestors to kings in the long duration
we are braiding their hair in the cathedral

my mother emails me that she won't press charges if
I just send her back the pain-pills I stole, no questions asked. dementia

is wild but predictable. I don't even like opiates
like all of you all do.

the hole in my soul is somewhere else, filled
by other things. my dad shot bb guns at the deer

that ate his roses, made me go stand in the yard
in 3 layers of parkas to make sure it wouldn't

hurt the deer that bad. you can buy coyote piss
in the garden section at Home Depot or Lowe's, did you

know that. the first orchards
on earth, and what it meant to tend them

Willie Nelson says when both your parents die
then you are an orphan. time

is all we have. it is all we have ever had. Jeff
made fry-bread last night, his mom's recipe, said

when she makes it it puffs up a lot bigger. "time," I say,
"in baking has to be treated as another ingredient."

a quantity of time same as an amount of sugar or flour or baking powder
his mom lives on a reservation in Nebraska. "I didn't

know anywhere could be that FLAT," he says. I drank
two bottles of wine. I'm only a little ashamed to admit it and now

it is raining and the whole world is shining and wet and beautiful
so bless the yeasts and bless the grapes and forgive ourselves

as we trespass into the future together
not one of us asked to be born. that is not

how it works. we are all a function
of a desire that preceded us, since the first.

"Another experimental method for
storing data in DNA, reported by
Harvard scientists in 2017, involves
feeding fragments of nucleotides
to an already existing DNA strand
in a living cell, which incorporates
the DNA fragments as an immune
defense mechanism. The team
inserted Eadweard Muybridge's
1878 film clip of a galloping
horse into a bacterium. 'The
trace is left in a living organism,'
says Milenkovic. As long as
that organism exists, including
its offspring, the information is
stored–although it may become

mutated over time, altering the
information."

the horses that galloped once, gallop on in our endless soul
they are mutating as they gallop ; mid-stride, into another dimension

someday there will be no more horses
and there never was such a thing as a soul

my mother emails me back "found some of the missing pills
I'm sorry I accused you.... the one of 7.5 billion people I love best"

I order seven
million nematodes
online

to harness
the universe
is a myth
of tool-use,
awake
to the filaments and
wires of time
flailing about
making things
and why not

how nice it is to have the right
tool for the job, hammer, tiller, spatula, impact
driver, pesticide, 7/16ths wrench, excavator,
ride-share app, internet, I love you all

all of us, just bugs in our
small communion glass, so pour us out

in the pink
aphid fields of the universe

roll over,
stars

found some of the missing pills

SLOW DOWN WITH THESE SERENE CITY-BUILDING GAMES

cities: braille
cities: teeth
cities: complex molecular arrangements

as if the earth itself had a love for geometry, as if
the earth itself believed in time, dimensional
interiority, the reflective properties of glass
"that I may see my face"

will we have made a more beautiful world?
first contact: "hey, I like what you've done with the place"

a blip in the organic biochemistry of surfaces
pinprick of spire and firelight; electrons forced to hum and glow
"energy, in physics, is the capacity to 'do work'" wire-light,
beam me up—dig me down—there is no other now than here

iSky iReason iSparrow iSeason, then
there was a small Greatness came up in me (in us
all together now: secrete a city, porous self, mind-
sieve, hold my memories, digital storage 100 gigabytes free
with premium service, Alexandria, archive and cipher of 3D-,
4D-, 5D-architecture to live inside. Another World
is Inevitable Actually—the starlings all turn together
in sunlight, then bank left come suddenly visible as shadow,
light, bits flicking on and off in the binary code, whole
flock of 'em gone pixel and silent, riding the dis-
equilibrium of air, heat transfer, awareness—your brain is
expensive, in some sense, so feed it the shimmering fats and
complex sugars as it creates the thermogenesis of your attention,
the recursive circuit the world asks of you, feed it.

"in an artificial hibernaculum" the cold demigods wake, numbers
glittering in the crystal lattice of their thousand million
bazillion quadrillion eyes

Universe Today's Nov 4th Newsletter :
"EVEN MORE PILLARS OF CREATION!"

O monkey
playing in the interstice, O aliens,
O self-aware AI undressing
in the mainframe, perplex't
as I too am perplex't, awed, squinting
at the grainy image, refresh
the page, the grainy word emerges,
the electrons build on the mineral surface
the carbon atoms walk across the surface
the lithium ions flash in the diagram
like they're dancing, this is an error code, this
is an error code, I can feel it, awake

a volt is a jewel of work
a nine-volt battery can provide nine joules of work

either way my deep cycle marine RV battery won't work so I walk
down from the neck of the lake into the dried-up lakebed,
stand in a time fractal with last year's me in a canoe over my head

the mud cracked like ancient dinosaur scales, the back of some giant
being heaved up. I can see how veins of ore would fill in cracks like these
if there was a running molten sea of something flooding over us

something red leaking in the effluvia, fanning out, oxidized iron
bleached bare and tangled tree roots, old tires, rivulets cut channels
in the mud, the distant water still distant, my dogs zooming joyful
on the far expanse. small plants starting to grow, fox sedge and little
willows, some purple spotted knobby grasses, the seeds
must've been buried in the silt, I think, washed down
the branching watershed. it is grey and chilly and beautiful
I walk almost forever, the lake a distant shimmer the mud
dry under my boots the clouds in time-lapse over us, dried cup of sky
I walk until I have to turn back in the thickening dark

    some leaves an undulating red
    ribbon on the turquoise below

I pick up a dead minnow white against the dark rocks—
"an offering." I think… "no" I think…that would mean
I am the god—"instead, maybe…" I think "…a gift?"

blue fishing pole, hook through the gills of the dead minnow
catch a few yellow-bellied perch and one smallmouth bass in eden

    big boulders the muscles of some sleeping
    geometric god reflected in the blue pools
    transformers crouched in the matrix
    suspended in time's solution

now a deeper dusk: the twinkle of lights come on on the far ridge
up past the long blue throat of the creek, that'll be

Bernie and Todd's house, and Matt's, the crisscross
low hill's shoulders in the haze. I walk up the white stones
toward them, smoke one last cigarette as the moon
comes miraculously out, lake fort smith says moonlight
is a grave, and time has its grace of us, think
for the first time in my life that I'm grateful
to the universe for making me a being to be
aware of it, follow the path of moonlit leaves through
dark trees to my truck, which miraculously starts

now me and the car in front of me are on a lit night highway
in a video game the road laid along the curvature of the world

now I am on the top of the ridge, past the new turkey house, past
the big pond and the dead tree where the killdeer used to live, two horses
in a yard and the whole dark valley to my right falling off below, past
Matt working on his dump-truck by LED spotlight, I can see
the knuckled long arm silhouette of the excavator, gentle
beast machine with its cradle-claw, crack
open a beer the long driveway up the moon

may time be more gentle with us next year
maybe tomorrow it will rain. claw-hands
of the giant tractor of the universe holding us,
hauling us along

> "lol I've seen it lower" texts Billy, "whenever
> they drained shepherd springs down to build up the lake"
>
> and Carson: "isn't that the drinking water for the city?"
> "where we're not allowed to swim?"
>
> (where we always swim, the green water and the alcove with the
> skull)

what is or isn't shared, it's not nothing, actually

"typically, there's an inverse relationship between the dollar and industrial metals" today: "a 12% rally in the price of copper" & "debt grew at its fastest rate in 15 years"

"some users may experience a harmless tingling"

coming across the word "antinomian" in reference to Sufi mystics in the introduction to Farid Ud-Din Attar's *The Conference of the Birds*. Google: "Antinomian–relating to the view that Christians are released by grace from the obligation of observing the mortal law." I frown in disgust, pivot, examine the antinomianism of my anarchism through this prism now—

"A young Iranian man accused of lighting a trash can on fire during a protest could face death row for 'waging war against God' and 'corruption on earth,'" the article in Radio Free Europe says

"however inaccurate the Bohr model might be, it will do for our description of electricity," the engineer on YouTube says

the Mississippi moves about 60% of the U.S.'s grain shipments bound for overseas: corn, wheat, soybeans, oats   goodbye, goodbye, goodbye—

the Mississippi is drying up. old cars, old engine parts, broken bottles, rotting fish, sneakers, leaking car batteries, plastic bags shredded and caught in bent or broken branches, sprouting willows, cracked mud. Marc says it happened once when he was little in Memphis and his parents took him to walk out on it

catfish fillets fried in the late afternoon light and the glowing strands of time

the electrons gather at the southern gate
the electrons crest the ridge overlooking the valley
the quarks start spinning where there was once
a tall-grass prairie and now there are high rises and
superhighways to the traffic-jammed heart
of the infinite city, which is my heart
and all the hearts of men, electromagnetic
rubber and pinging off the satellites in low-earth orbit

presumably the quarks are turning in your heart
as they were in the endless ocean, the first frost
the next spring, matter can neither
be created nor destroyed, they say
and yet here we are in the hologram with death
who is always beside us

a child walks out into the universe

voltage equals current times resistance
I turn the light on in a small room

"I was an object of time, filled with dread," Lyn Hejinian writes

inkblot faraday, far away soul over cage,
faraway soul over ocean, faraway soul divided by satellite,
faraway location of joy. there are whole fields of sadness.
this won't last forever. it is a question of endurance
cupping the warmth in your small hands.

rotational motion 'round electrical wire
polarized battery earth alternating current
earth will you be the ampules to my voltage
the structure of our rhyme the inter-
dimensional folding of our net?

the work of my net's dominion
all life is a game played by a bored electrical field
eons of static. you there in the back, make some noise

the crush of angels, the sound of water, electric
hymnal of the night sky, bless

the bitcoin mining farms have relocated to the sheer drop
and rush of Niagara Falls for cheap biodynamic hydroelectric energy,
the article says, the "haunting hum" of the huge fans keep people awake
they are suing the bitcoin factories on account of the noise—

permission to sauté the pink
souls of the frozen shrimp in butter
and Walmart olive oil that's probably
not olive oil. exhale, tilt left, one for sorrow,
bacon fat, inhale, come center, molecule-transfer
phase transition—in my mind,
in my mind's eye I can see it now

the shrimp are singing in the sea
the hydrothermal vents will sing to me
as if I were more or less than a vortex of time
consuming smaller vortices of time
the big kitchen of time with all the light
in it the steam the sound of voices…

I email my mother "I feel like I'm running up an
endless wheel that keeps spinning faster, will it feel like this
forever?"

"the heart is an electric organ," the article
about lightning strikes says. "thunderbolts
are like big batteries….the air around a lightning
bolt can be hotter than the surface of the sun"

> "Nerves, blood and
> muscles—because
> of their high water
> content—are the
> body's best conductors
> of electricity, and
> therefore more
> vulnerable to
> lightning. Bones and
> fat are relatively poor
> conductors. Skin ranks
> in between."

error: something went wrong with the Galaxy Store. please check
your connection or try again later. the man on the radio asks
whether or not the internet is "digital commons" or "a landscape
of information warfare" : in which dimension do these worm-holes exist?
the star-nosed mole of our eyes fondling objects in the interstice
touching them, squeezing them gently, choosing what to put
back into the fold and what to take out and eat

full of significance and beauty : fish skin   brain-stem   catechism
what is belief?   go vote on Mount Comfort Road   go catch some fish

relationship of gun [to] belief, of fragility [to] violence
number of 50 cent goldfish we poured out in Lake Wilson : 31
number of fish we caught at Lake Wilson : 0
number of snapping turtles we watched hunt
the shining 50 cent goldfish in the shallow weeds
at Lake Wilson : a lot
waiting for the dogs to come back

relationship of belief [to] what-is-real
inverse (?) relationship of fear [to] belief

all knowledge is only a current model: database, simulation

the tiny PetSmart goldfish glowing so bright in the murky
water little orange-gold flames bright as beacons
"I'm alive" "I'm alive" "I'm alive" I'm cold in the new
water, a "flash" in "the pan"

next time I'll spring for the $1.50 ones, I say, they are
bigger. you want to give what you love at least
a chance at surviving out there

to behold [in some relation to] to reveal
a universe in which all the dogs come back, worn out
from running, joyful, a universe in which they get given half my
fried chicken and taken home to a soft couch, bless

"today is beautiful!" framed on the wall
at my dentist's office where she takes
X-rays of my teeth

where I lie in the chair that cradles me with a flat-screen TV
on a robotic arm in position above my eyes and a remote control
in my lap I choose "PLANET EARTH AT NIGHT" the glowing elephants
on the infrared-thermal-heat camera bellow and stomp in my headphones
the women pass shining autoclaved tools back and forth over me they are
talking and laughing about things in their life the tiniest needle
in the universe pulses something numbing into my cheek, bless

the filling takes 20 minutes, and I walk out into the sunlit parking lot.
it cost 500 dollars.

on my way home I stop at the gas station and run into Matt filling up
the dozer he says he has to get all his teeth pulled and get dentures he is 31

another year "around the sun" they say

what is or isn't shared   and who you share it with
a day is set aside for memory   like this we are a vessel

you have to tune yourself to the frequency
and let it lead you around like a bull in a pasture
in a valley between the blue mountains where the great
city will be built along the river beneath the stars

electric hem electric shroud

bots are gathering at the western gate
they are singing a weird hymn there

"there's a lot of legacy hardware
going into this rocket launch"

god—it will be beautiful, throwing trash out of our ark-ship like scripture,
decipher us, upward, outward, we carry our myths into the universe, which
was made for us, which was made in our image

just kidding, you anomaly of the void hairless all weird noses, eyebrows, esophagi, limbs, genitals and all; you grew here on accident. you will never be more beautiful than you are now. hold up the mirror of glass, phosphorus and sky, silicon hardware, membranous fold. maybe tomorrow. grotesque cul-de-sac android of some inconceivable future grace.

> "earlier this year an artificial
> intelligence program called
> AlphaFold, developed by
> the Google-owned company
> DeepMind, predicted the 3-D
> structures of *almost every known*
> *protein*—about 200 million in
> all."

I divide 12 by 7 on Google to see how many hours per day I spent on my phone last week "12/7" : Google says: "Matthew 12:7: I desire mercy, not sacrifice" fuck

"imagine two people, in the void of space, playing catch with a ball" starts the YouTube video on electromagnetic fields (they get further and further away from each other as the energy transfers from the thrown ball to their bodies, back and forth in the void of space)

I Google: is the earth a battery

voltage is a differential: the cooler air sinks, the warmer air rises,
the whole thing churns, turbulent flow, liminal vortices, call it life—
vivify it—

300 handfuls of thunder and a god-sized bucket of rain dumped
over the surface, today

sunflower growing in the window pot from bird seed
the birds must've dropped, 40lb bag of black oil sunflower seeds

from tractor supply, bless

do my exercises along with the YouTube lady, bless

what is at stake here? it is my mind
and all the minds of men

we are each holding a piece of the net

stitch ourselves into the world, hold it open,
receive it

become known to the universe, inverse relation,
so flex your soul, like this.

click open your durational attention with one swipe
to attend to all the things that need attending to

it's not going to perceive itself now is it

train your muscles in the data stream, you will only
be alive once so you may as well enjoy it, the irrefutable
physicality of being, to walk over the surface
for a while, the while that you have

the knees that you have, the shoulder joints that you have
the lungs that you have, each incalculable calculation in you, the
mitochondria are the powerhouse of the cell, Sara's nursing instructor in
Arkansas looked up at the ceiling and apologized to god for saying knees
were a bad design, bless

make meatballs in the cast iron with the radio on
tomatoes grown in some summer fields somewhere
open up a can of somewhere else, a record of sunlight and labor
whatever a small offering is, offer it

Neurohacker.com [in some
relation to] biomimicry : "out
of the mockingbirds
throat, the musical shuttle," robotic

moth-wing-eye-spot-big-and-dark o fool me slow-
wing-blink the "expanded payload ecosystem" what
is at stake here: the organism in a dream
dream-sense pulled from non-sense, blue
threads, pink, bio-chemical scents, the sensors
all respond to painful stimulus on the surface of the blue-
green planet, robotic-wingspan mechanisms sail
off the highest cliffs, like this. what is pain [in some
relation to] sentience, first known
feeling first felt. so shock me, awe or electric
outlet, our internet loves
the aphids who tend it.

to suckle, sure, and before the flood. there were
roses, sure, and laughter—but that was new—and
precious. would you have been the one to sing that
first hymn? statistically, unlikely, the guttural
echo, the high-pitched call, the grunt and shove, a little
murmuring, the coming storm

"can't carry a tune in a bucket" they say
"kinship identification rituals" they say
slow down the time-sequence of birdsong,
whale songs travel the whole length
of the whole ocean, they say

the whales are building sonic maps inside the ocean, they say, they can hear
each other over the whole cubic distance, wavelengths long as a football
field, if you can believe it

mechanized tool use [in some relation to] elision of time, space
I fly on an airplane north, [my] time contracts over the racing ground

they are up here terraforming Idaho below
the periwinkle mountain ring

hiking on the Talus-fields of the moon with Sara, "melon-ball"
boulders from "the Bonneville Flood" 15,000 years ago, following
horseshoe prints in the moon-dust, imagining a future earth

"over the sterile sands and the fields beyond, where the child..."

the humpback whales are contemplating mortality
in the planet earth's wine dark oceans, they are passing the body
back and forth between them, on the radio, below the pink-
white mountain range, we traverse the geometric plain, 65mph, some
black cattle in a feedlot, mud, sagebrush, a thing too big, we fly along
the rocks, the sky, the river carved at the end of the last ice age, which
was very recent in the huge history of time, glaciation, whole coursing
thing of it the glint and flood, our eyes are tired. it is all too big.
fractal rock-cliff-ribbon rising edge of world, one hawk
banks against the driving wind, the streaming light floods in—
go home and make dinner all together in a warm room
while the wind whips and the world freezes over outside

what is at stake here, bleak
algorithm, a tended garden, a few sensors
scattered across the surface, reflect, face
of my face, changing with the seasons, rhyme
of all with all, mitochondrial Eve first mother, a footstep
in mud, a record of mammal warmth and how to carry something fragile
carefully into the future, where it will be changed, where it will be
more beautiful, more vital, more alive

stop trying to enchant the world, Cody. it is dull and gray and full of dismal people stuck in the relentless inherited reactive-emotion cycles of their maladapted ancestors, of their shrieking and angry and probably scared lineage, panic, anger, impulse, lash out, pass the pain down, daisy chain, each to each, mothers, fathers, state-sanctioned caretakers, someone yelling on the subway. Rene with her finger in my face at Jeff's house yelling, a grown-ass woman yelling, whoever did this to everyone, all insane, dumb volatility all the way back, cruelty, careless negligence, the absurdity, the blind oblivious embarrassing rage, the petty vicious hostilities of wounded animal's first animal sin.

grow up everybody, we are all so sick of this, each reinscribing these self-replicating cyclic entrenchments, there is no forward, there is no future, it just goes on over and over until everyone alive now finally dies, but the thing's been done. there will always be new children, it's been passed down, vertical-pain transfer of genetic lineage. soon it will be over. the other animals will go back to killing each other in peace. there will be lava and ice floes and sea lion pups ripped limb from limb in the cold ocean and dragonflies hovering above a summer lake. let the people say stupid, untrue, and horrible things back and forth to each other, Cody. let her throw that wrench at your bare toes every day, who cares, small meanness, necessity, this stale and sour and urgent entity of grief beating around our heads with a million entropic wings. only I am real, each person says, I can see only me, reality is a myth, no one else exists, if we could only see it, if we could only open up the window, we could shoot it out of the sky. speak, sentience, is this the best you've got? for us? around and around we go, the imbecilic unweavers of this rotten, fraying net.

Catabasian, get some rest. the road is long and getting longer. the filaments are sparking on the sea. it is raining in Arkansas.
what was once will never

tender of

who will win the golden testicle?
your portal verification code is []

o this magnetic
transcriptase has conspired, you know,
to hold us, gently or not, in its green
and vibrating rings.

"it would have been beautiful" if we had instead been
inimitable dew, or pathogens, the color of water before
the first flood, dust, or various other things.

now it is December. chickadees and goldfinches
at the feeder in the grey mist, chickadees and goldfinches
all the same. the electric birdbath keeps the water from freezing over.
this is what love is. they have fracked out
the crude oil for this. I don't
know what to say.

"[the poet] judges not as the judge judges but as the sun falling round a helpless thing" writes Whitman—but it is us, old man, who are helplessly falling 'round the sun, like this. [and then there was 4.5 billion years of plummeting] [one more year to go I say] [I judge the angle of the sun]

one theory is that the first
tools were likely not spears
and arrows but instead
baskets and nets, to carry
things in or to trap small
animals, fish. to free up
our hands, which can only
hold so many things. a
surplus, what is more than
our immediate hands can
carry—

we are saving some grapes
for later; wait, they have
undergone a *change*—

from a book on weaving
baskets: "More than mere
containers, baskets, like
their creators are what is
*in*side as well as what is
*out*side" and later "weaving
is an art of rhythm, form,
and time"

the oscillating helix of the battery of time, and me.
the ship of death is late. there are "supply chain issues"
I place my order with the void and pray.

it is with the weight of a feather
measured against prayer, or laughter   it is a blue
gem   ice cold   there are no fields of heaven
you have to choose whom to forgive   carefully
nothing ceases to exist   this is crucially important
you have only one shot at this   pull yourself together, Cody
the first seeds were hard and bitter   the one life you have to live

after all, this is your one and only life, you may as well
learn to enjoy it

when you get home Marc will make you a cheesecake and you will survive
the winter.

the horses stomp in the fields of heaven, they do not stomp for thee.

I gather honeysuckle vines along the creek, alone,
and you come with me

WATCH THESE RARE OCEAN CREATURES CAUGHT
ON CANDID ROBOT CAMERA

THE DIRTY ROAD TO CLEAN ENERGY; HOW THE ELECTRIC
VEHICLE BOOM IS RAVAGING THE ENVIRONMENT

Nicolai Tesla's father wanted him to be a priest, [thus] he became an engineer

they are strip mining for nickel in Sulawesi, they are earth-blasting for cobalt in the Congo, "In Chile, huge evaporation pools draw lithium out of the salt flats of the Atacama Desert." prices for these minerals are "soaring." O eagle of my same heart, is this how you make a battery? Okay, pinnacle of man, end-game of the species, storage-cell of the past into the future, voltage meter of my same charged soul, vast and trunkless legs of steel will power up in the desert, streamlined recursive non-consciousness of our next being, Large Millimeter Array [in what] relationship of Awe to Despair in the electric sensors, store up some awe for me, O oscillating thing.

ritual motion around a center, this is how a battery works.
mitochondria press protons across a fatty membrane, charged
acid of the first ectoplasmic urge, this is how you do work: each
electron a seed carried along in the current

vinegar : diode : soul
joules heaped up on joules, whole piles of them

a cache: a logical pyramid, a nest
a cache: a hole in the ground where we store
what is more than we can carry, where it rots, memory
a place for what is left over once the calculations
are done: zero out the zero-sum and what remains
is the whole world of moving things, no rest
in the thermodynamic flow, sunlight, coffee-cup, radiant
body, swapping electrons through daily ritual, motion
of touch, spark plug, myelin sheath, where we store

the shining fats for future thought, because we love
our future self, all our future's selves fractal outward, this
dominion of earth piling up its electricity in us

it is different to enact a complex sequence
that's what I learned when I researched the difference between just
eating sugar and eating things that break down
into sugar   this is the space between

the universe appreciates a complex sequence
I pour battery acid into the six
cells of the 4-wheeler battery and connect
two alligator clip clamps on a drip
charge plugged into a wall outlet to the collective

hive mind burning coal or fracking oil
in Oklahoma and humming. I am redistributing
the pleasure circuitry of the world. I ride the 4-wheeler
"into the sunset." just kidding, I try
to be back home by dark, like the warm-
blooded, diurnal mammal I am

that the earth *caught life* as a planet might catch a virus
atmospheric oxygen, clear skies, blue seas… and bluer than blue,
what eyes, could see—it will strike us down

I gather honeysuckle vines for baskets while my dogs lie patiently in the leaves

the plans are in the works to grind up and 3D print the regolith on the moon
into a landing pad, roads, buildings. "this is how you know they're serious"
the Universe Today newsletter says, "when they start planning infrastructure"

"but fundamentally" Tor Norretranders writes, "the nonconscious body is not under the control of consciousness… The body is part of a biological metabolism with the living system on the planet—and this participation is not subject to the power of the consciousness. We do not have access, via the body's own means, to changing the role each of us plays on earth. We are part of a living system to which we are so adapted that there is no freedom to get off."

The Field of The World — today — 60°F day after days and days of rain, sun, steam off the creek, table, deck, dishes, tree trunks steaming, lichen and bark, wet leaves, trash — and all the amorous frogs belting out their hymns in grunts and groans this warm December morning — futile in some relation to joyful : futile in what relation to joyful

one planet: awake   glow worm of my same heart in the morning, wiggling, opening its photosensitive cell clusters we call eyes, the baritone toads by the green pond, one hawk circling the many little birds, all inquisitive, sensate, seeking —

more dire than myth   more sensate than science   more forgiven than iron
cobalt   silk   silos   lithium-ion   battery acid   milk   roots dug
up out of the dark earth forgiven by combine and grid   god damned city
of cables I love you   it is the first morning   forgiven here
give it back   I said   give it back

inverse relation; seeds [to] survival   viable planet   dandelion   amaranth
rabbit   tire-factory   satellites

what hubris: "a manifestation of the universal consciousness." shut up sweet hairless ape of my same hubris, we are just lucky to even get to chicken scratch out this tiny amount of perception; purple-finch claw wet bark some bugs a vague itch occasional desire a cool breeze maybe on a hot day or the opposite, love

tiny eyes, kaleidoscope; vast quanta of unsensed world, scrim of awareness
just right on the surface   barely even metabolic   who needs a brain
anyway   not me

fragmented, broken cup, disturbance in the flow
entropy increases in a closed system, but! our world is an open system

"thermodynamically speaking," says the book. so we aren't
really breaking any laws by being here. it is not even that improbable.

we are not even that miraculous, shining in the tiny sun that made us, going about our days.

we are holes in the universe
many holes, all at once.

strands of radiation flow around us
a cascade of impulse charges the net

whatever the caloric metabolism of a given planet, desire exists only in the distance between want and fulfilment, thermodynamically speaking.

55 Cancri e is so close to its star that "the surface of the planet is an ocean of lava and its interior may be filled with diamonds." Okay, nerd. that sounds fake. that sounds beautiful. it is thus the "dawn" of a "new day" on earth as it is on 55 Cancri e, a new day which can be calculated as an action potential or quantified as a cache of imagination-storage, a "unit" of "time" or just defined in terms of light hitting the surface, for a bit, like this. coming up over that hill there, sliding down these carbon-boned life forms we call trees.

the backward-forward arrow of memory to imagination
like this memory is reverse imagination in the entropic flow of time

flow back up, drop't
yolk tucked back in; kindness encased
swallowed, whole

Richard Feynman writes,
"The atoms that are in the
brain are being replaced;
the ones that were there
before have gone away. So
what is this mind of ours;
what are these atoms with
consciousness? Last week's
potatoes! They now can
remember what was going
on in my mind a year ago."

the joke goes: "I was born at night,
but I wasn't born *last* night". yes,
you were. human shaped luna moth of
non-functioning logic awake
in the automated substrata of eden's weird hallways
stumbling around, fooling cash registers
with your magnificent cerulean wings

time, they say, will tell.

the meme on the internet says "everything will be okay,
eventually, in thousands of years, for rocks."

"tomorrow," they say, "never comes"

the transistor radios of my heart just the same
shouldering their looped parallel cables into the apex of distance,
the transformers go marching, marching, "across
the fruitless plain" O Nebraska of America's harsh
winters, prospecting for a sense of place at the edges of the
known and unknown universe just the same.

sifting for diamonds at the Crater of Diamonds State Park,
just gravel and mud, dismal world stretching endless, furrowed into each direction, dug by the heavy machinery's metal teeth, churned earth, kinship

rituals of suffering together, the pouring rain, laughing late into the night, trying our best

what a family is, in each culture. what family is, to you.

weaving and unweaving the myth of coherence
weaving and unweaving the lineage of myth

direct current of one soul, alternating current
of many souls, go catch some beauty in the net
go out and have some fun, poet, if you can figure out how.

"in essence" the article says "the researchers are learning to build a second sun...[the announcement] was greeted with the requisite hosannas"

in his book *The User Illusion: Cutting Consciousness Down to Size,* Tor Norretranders describes the number of perceived sensations *discarded* by the body's sensory systems as giving rise to the much smaller amount of sense-data that comes into our consciousness. he talks about the amount of discarded information, or "exformation" in terms of *informational depth,* a sort multidimensional informational space shaped by the amount of sheared off data, that chasm that holds up the plateau in which our senses give rise to the sensation of being awake

maps work like this; out of the noise only salient features are highlighted

memory is a path back through the billowing static, narrow and branching, reaching out across the distance of all things

the dendrites light up in the chemical solution   describe the shape of known space   in your mind, in your mind's eye   I am waiting
the liquid fills the vessel   the electricity branches across it   I am reaching out   the delicate tendrils   lichen-consciousness in the interstitial light   aspic and fovea of distance I am boiling down the chicken of suffering   I am changing fats to glucose   in my mind
in my mind's eyes   in the bacteria of my gut's   grace or gaze   or pasture

the lights on in all the little houses by the small highway, a distant ache come wandering down the hills

just plant the ginger from the store, why not—its lineage going all the way back to the first   it will grow green shoots for you if you're lucky   it will bloom

"the future" the radio says "was invented 75 years ago today" [the segment is on transistors]   and then the whole world spread out before me   like a lesson or command

"the government is keeping the atomic clocks warm with a chicken egg incubator," the radio says. "time," the radio says, "is the least reusable commodity we have"

"you have to keep counting. if you stop counting, you don't know the time anymore," the man on the radio says

"this feels somehow Sisyphean…?" says the reporter

"you said it, brother" says the guy from the Department of Commerce, time division.

the time it takes to roll the whole universe   up a green hill somewhere
to calculate shipment deliveries   to green lawns America   to lay out
the green circuits   for fabrication   interlocked gear-chains
spreadsheets spread across the entire world   but do they enjoy it   coupling
and decoupling in the amniotic breeze

how much work to build the world   to count it all up   on your fat little
fingers   since the first   invent a technology that can count to more than
ten   and on your toes, grasping at twenty   climbing up a spire of the
mind   to hold the days in place   no stay there   time's ratchet   time's fly-
reel   a silver ball thrown back and forth between time's giant hands

"the wind's free orchestra" Whitman writes

a voltage is a difference outside of equilibrium

waterwheel on a sun-flood day, bright as becoming, the new technologies: are you purposefully not understanding me?

day bright as a bell
day my small allotment of sun
ease-of-use [] a space of time
[a space held outside of time, for us]

I think in order for artificial intelligence or robots to be considered alive they would have to have the capacity to feel pain, which is the manifestation of an excruciating need to not be in pain, which is the expanded-field substrate in which a sense of self can start to exist—put differently, what would self-compel an AI, or an embodied robotic intelligence, into interacting and moving around in meaningful ways—why move at all? the two horses, pleasure and pain, drive the motile mechanism in order to carry forward that life inside it—

"and yet, it moves" murmurs Galileo,
being led out of the courtroom.

"steerable eyes" "gratitude" "remote presence" I am in
the room with you. ring-camera, I can feel your heart beating,
the rise and fall of your chest with each breath, these are known
things. is this grace. the robotic spider eyes are watching you. Alexa,
remind me that all eyes are the eyes of god, awake

technically the sun is a plasma. whatever that means. this
is a gentle reminder. this is a known phenomenon. this is
sometimes too much to bear. and yet we do bear it. separate
and also together. the information superhighway is at my fingertips
and inside my brain. we tesseract and falter there. we call our mother.
freezing is a phase transition in the molecular state of water. Alexa,
remind me I need to order a 3-phase converter for my soul.

in some places batteries are called "dry cells" to distinguish them
from the electricity grid, which is conceived of as current, as flow,
a liquid electric river running between us

like this metaphor pours itself out for us
the big dipper, the silver spoon

the hydrocarbons of the moon

the same river, many times, differently, or the opposite
I don't know, the battery acid in the river, the fish of my same heart
which is the heart of my country

> "birds can fly. airplanes can fly. airplanes do not
> fly exactly as birds do" writes Rodney Brooks
> "we are careful to remember that they are not
> flapping their wings or burning sugar in their
> muscles—they do not even have muscles. but
> they do fly;" the comparison will be set up
> between animal/human and machine/robot
> emotions…the next chapter is titled *Specialness*—
> O no.

from an article on concrete about a massive hydroelectric dam in the Alps: "For more than a decade, through snow and rain and fog, the workers poured that thick grey mixture day after day after day, and gradually a monolith began to rise between the mountains." and "One booklet described it as a 'concrete temple enthroned in a mineral universe'"

I buy two books on Ebay:

The Machine in the Garden: Technology and the Pastoral Ideal in America

and

The Garden in the Machine: The Emerging Science of Artificial Life

"if it keeps up like this the power lines'll go down" texts Jeff, about the freezing rain. "if you need anything, yell"

the wind, it is howling. "increased demand on the electric grid." carpet of snow-quilted country. I fill up two 5-gallon water jugs and a lot of empty wine bottles with water and think about batteries in relation to memory and time

"the sacrifice zone" "climate controlled storage unit" "homo sacre" the flowers of my country. "indivisible" "for all"

"Last year's Infrastructure Report Card for the U.S. graded much of the country's concrete infrastructure—roads, dams, airports, stormwater systems, inland waterways—as a D, meaning poor, at-risk and exhibiting significant deterioration."

my pipes freeze at 2pm the faucet wide open. feeding the glowing woodstove split oak firewood I cut last week, pumping out just enough heat to keep this one parcel of warm space warm, inside of the outside of the world, the energy input to maintain this peculiar goldilocks disequilibrium. pink spun fiberglass and compressed particle board membrane, pink satin real-tree fabric over the cat door, ice crystals on the windowpanes where no god of any warm-blooded creatures peers in

gestate in your own womb, ice world

we can talk functionally about the metabolism of any living system, house, city, planet. we need to think about inputs and outputs. in biochemistry, metabolism can either be directed toward expendable energy or toward growth but not at the same time. how small the world contracts. each motion is a choice, one thing, or another. how crystalline, the structure, emerge!

tonight it is going down to -7°F with a windchill of -25°, the weather app says. people will die tonight in Fayetteville. people will freeze to death in tents and encampments off the bike path, in unheated houses and trailer houses and apartments north of the highway, in Prairie Grove or Siloam Springs, Hog-Eye, Chester, Mountainburg, tarps over the roof, the cold pouring all the way down the river valley as if it itself were a river. I hope they have wine or a strong whiskey for it, centers of warmth, cradled, the denser, heavy air, Y-city, Texarkana, Pine Bluff...

energy, in physics: the capacity to do work [or] produce heat
incandescent: the carbon skeletons held in congealed time
crystal matrix, sugar, sun, protons, photons, burn.
plug me into an outlet, keep me warm.

bury deep ye tubers of the mind
against the howling wind

in answer to the question "what, then, is
an emotion?" the neuroscientist Joseph
le Doux responds: "It's a conscious
awareness that something psychologically
or biologically important is happening to
you. Evolution gave us these behavioral
responses to stimulus, but those are not
yet emotions."

another article: "consciousness began
when the gods stopped speaking." I don't click on it.
I can't really take this anymore actually.

all night I hear Matt with the dozer piling gravel up in the creek bed.

hold this jar up gold against the blue the blur of
more tender to might around so so be of

and, causal, fold

analogous homonym: a rupture in the void where time grew all these inflorescences inside it, crustal, oily, fats shining in the splashing plasmid light, O

driving south down highway 71: Orion's belt directly vertical to the road. its three stars over the headlight-bare-tree-limb cathedral. a few house lights on in the dark distance and low hills. Marc texts me, "I just read this thing. that made me. maybe, for the first time, kind-of wish I could live for a really long time. how if the whole of human history. was an 800 page book. and if each page. was like a description. of 200 years increments. so. the first 799 pages would be in the dark. with like. no electricity," and, "I know you'll say. duh? but. it was momentarily fascinating." yes. it was momentarily. fascinating. someone pull the pull-start motor of my soul—

the propane heater coil glows
what it feels like to be alive

wherever you are,
today.

today's biotech companies, today's baby formula factories, fragility of the U.S. power grid. Venture capital. multi-nationals. mRNA vaccines. which symphony, this. permission to watch the erector set erect the world. obligate-symbiont, obligate-awareness, obligate-kinship, obligate-disavowal of care. Apple-Cash. "all investment carries the risk of loss." permission to never grow old. the work of one's body. the work of many hands. "Imagine the possibilities if you could undo the gene that is responsible for…" I put on spf 30 sunblock and stand naked in the sun.

SpaceWeather newsletter: "15 times black holes surprised us in 2022" I click on it

from here to Galilee beam me up, Nikolai take me with you
feed me the small fruits of some other brighter sun and acid rain furrowed land

terra informatis: grotesque palindrome: small ark
ache, acre, arc, or harbor—O Galileo, let down your hair
on that small island, a bigger beak—

who is it that is singing

"[OpenAI's computer programed chatbot's] responses read like a [person] who only knows the world through reading about it on the internet. Worse, it replies with unflinching certainty, even when writing absolute nonsense"

and

"If DNA is the code of life, then outfits like GeneArt are printshops—they synthesize custom strands of DNA and ship them to scientists, who can use the DNA to make a yeast cell glow in the dark, or to create a plastic-

eating bacterium, or to build a
virus from scratch"

Tor Norretranders writes "the simulation of the world is replacing the world"
I check the weather app to see if I am cold

and Ammons: "anybody doesn't believe in / reality should
/ try to start a dead car / on a 10-degree / morning"

where is the world's interface? take me to it.
I have a swiveling wrench set. I have an impact driver,
a pry bar, a soldering gun, a welding machine. I have
a sharp vinegar, tweezers, a teeth-whitening kit, a vise-
grip, a 5-gallon jug of gasoline, fake olive oil, two-stroke
engine oil, a little lubricant, a pack of 6 lighters, a handful
of sunflower seeds, a butane torch,
and strong heart. I think
we ought to at least try to do something

Marc is making lasagna and bringing me a beer the city water is still running in Fayetteville, Arkansas, sing to us through all the pipes in the city we will call it an orchestra we will hear a distant soprano we will say a few blessings for everyone to be safe we will walk the dogs down the bike path in the snow and pools of lamplight after my shower like we do every year we will call it a celebration

I don't know how to wire up the intricate
diodes, the green circuit boards of the future,
to mutate into a more beautiful coefficient
fuel efficient 5th-dimensional
fragment of the universe, cell
division-long-as-time, growing
old in the interstice—

"on the wing" "on the line"

what is or is not left to chance

there has to be a place the filaments touch the earth
to accept the infernal charge

I have a tap-and-die set
to widen all the holes

I know how to set cement,
the "pillars" of "creation"

I know how to angle
the disc grinder of the soul

to facet the faces of god
to polish a cold hard stone

to tape a few wires together
"cathode" or "salvation"

the stars all night, turning in their sockets
diesel for their kingdoms; the diaphanous wings
of the solar array unfurl in its circumpolar orbit
the gentle nonsentience of lab-grown meat
breathing in hydrogen, helium, oxygen, fermenting
cellulose structures built of sunlight, halogen, fixing
sugars in the cellular matrix, fixing
the carburetor before dark

you enkidu-android of programmed behavioral patterns, the code's been running rough since those first chords of chordate dawn, recalibrate the godparameters for us, archetype-human, objective morality of the striped fishing spider, extravagant sexuality of the red-assed baboon, the beautiful blue face-paint, the bowerbirds of world-building, what love is, beauty of the dung-beetle's green-gold carapace in the endless sewers of heaven, I'm with you, Sagittarius A* in the network of myth, I'm with you, walking the lit gridworks of the universe, stepping along the strings of light, Tulsa, Los Angeles, Manhattan, let's go out to dinner.

let's order meat flown in from the heartland, fish shipped in from the coasts. I'm with you paying credit card bills online to an automated system with a human female voice. sing to me, you robot lady. tell me which button to press. I'm with you sending digital cash on an app on my phone to a friend for yesterday's french fries, for ketamine.

(thank you) for electricity, what in the world is going on here, I'm with you standing somewhere at the dim interstice between the world and the world, vise-grip in hand, the keystone held in place by pure physics, gravity, the pressure the world exerts on the world, I'm with you in this brute physicality, sensuous and rough, bopping along these trajectories like sensate idiots, the satellites crash on the moon.

we are in the perpetual sequence of the future; are you coming with me; I want you to come with me; can you hear the huge gears turning; "have thy tools ready;" the hydrogen is combusting in the beautiful sun; the traffic on the highway spills over late into the evening; the airplanes are blinking overhead, each to each; the air-traffic controller is speaking the necessary ritual words, kneel down; the codes are chiseled in stone—the biochemical fugue, the redundant chorus the crocus hopeful; it springs eternal, the bioelectric signature, the frogs, awake.

like this memory is a continual calibration

"To me the single most important reason is that without AI alignment, AI systems are reasonably likely to cause an irreversible catastrophe like human extinction."

"2023 is set to be the hottest year on record." da **da** da **da** da **da** da **dum**

what is the biggest threat, today?

earthquakes in the Permian basin Texas oil fields, "the dawn
of the fracking boom" inland sea. I google "what was Texas like
in the Permian?" "the Permian ended in the Greatest Mass Extinction
Of All Time." okay, show off. "Kansas was unbearably hot 270 million years ago." honestly, in my experience, Kansas is sometimes still unbearably hot. lakes of evaporating brine, the long silences between periods of life, barcode and spectroscopy, geologic time.

I accept digital tracking in order to look at pictures of the volcanic surface of Mercury, digital tracking in what relation to memory's inscription, "I was here," we say to the internet, here is a memory. "on this day five years ago:" your last dog, the sun in her eyes, poised ready to jump after a stick I'm about to throw in the blue creek. that one might "accept" one's "death" in the face of things—that one might see one's death reflected back by that other face of things her golden eye her flexéd limbs

that one never dies in the digital interface, just erode as bits back
into digital soil, digital creek, digital sky, recombinant glitch of a future
megaworldtropolis, universe-soul, digital wineglass sparkling pink in
digitallightshaft off digital river, time flows us.

Venus was once a more habitable planet than earth but here we are, bastard child planet, doing the best we can with what we have been given

"After the sun reached a certain level of
brightness… the process became irreversible. The
oceans completely boiled off, solar radiation split
water into hydrogen and oxygen, the hydrogen
escaped into space, and the oxygen either escaped
along with it or got swallowed up by surface
minerals. The result is the dried-out hellhole we

see today." O Goldilocks, O Galileo, O Apollo
1 through 12, O Discovery, O small amphibians
exploring the incline of a slimy shore, O lapped
rock record of the shallow inland ocean, Ozarks,
on the hill across from me where the little lizards
rest on moss on rocks on earth, O today, O the
Mars rover going silent its solar cells covered in
dust.

Happy Birthday Curiosity. O memory, O new
mutants blinking awake, O gene-transfer of ache
to ache or whatever else this life is made of sing us
a little song how old are you today Perseverance,
endurance, O Captain, my—it is this life,

this life or any other

walking along the regolith pink in the sunset, sweetgum balls
spiked in silhouette tree scaffold, limb eyelash dendritic of dark creek,
reach the far reach, the mars rover in the distance gathers
mars rocks by LED light through dark trees, I see it

the congealed light, which is memory
black hill the sky a lighter black, which is a texture

then—torn ligament of yellow feather something
—I guess—ate the body left this wing I spread the feathers out
like fingers on rocks in this the last light on earth

the beast machine its gentle teeth graze skin of earth, like this
the beauty in the machine, awake

blasphemy in the chain of being
exultation in the chain of being
boring simple rituals in the chain of being
fatty-acid chains of being, survival-odds of seed pods,
of protein-bonds and soul, metabolized order, anti-theogonies
in the chain of being, particle, participle, citizen, plasma,
indulgence. are you a human being reading
this? augmented with robotics? stem-cells?
CRISPR gene edited genes? vaccinated? did you
download your memory to your phone's camera's
data storage chip? upload it to the cloud? do you
still have the cloud in the time you are in? or do you
have some new multi-valent atmosphere? do you share it
with friends or family across the globe or global network?
is this what love is? what would you do to extend your one
and only life, take vitamins? minerals? eat the leafy greens
grown in the agricultural sector of Eden, California? drink
the steeped beans of cleared jungle? elevate your heart rate
by jumping up and down like an idiot for two whole minutes?

my silly mostly hairless ape family full of sadness, gazing
out at a sunset from a high rock somewhere? can you feel the planet turning,
sometimes, in the morning? what would it have meant

to have made a more beautiful world? first there was the stillness,
then there was the breaking. have you created the new kinship rituals
of the internet? eaten the new meat of non-sentience grown in the cool
glass bowls of a manufactured heaven? drank the fermented juice
of the beautiful new fruits glowing their new colors in the dark?
I still have just the same old fruits, here. I scoop the orange flesh,
the swollen seeds, the hopeful tendrils and the earnest sprouts
I say to them, "you will grow in a bucket by the window." I will give
you this, I press them down, white knuckle of garlic green at the tip,
fractal potato-eye, ginger-bud almost breaking through the thin skin.
it is raining tonight in Arkansas, January 2, 2023. I set
the God-parameter to 0 and go dice onions in the swirling universe

we can only metabolize
the material of our own
pasture—horizon—enclosure
shudder or shatter
city block—tarmac or rolling acre
the glass half catches us,
our image—the sky
slinking along the corridors
of human-made thought

got home late, drunk, ate 3 pieces
bacon in the skillet, plucked hot
from spitting fat, burnt the tips
of my fingers one perfect thing

von Uexkull says an animal's body
is like a house "with many sensory windows
overlooking an outlying garden"

even I can't talk about the slaughterhouses of eden

"A 4-pound piece of eye
round or loin trimmed of
fat and sinew"

BIRDS SING TO THEIR EGGS, AND THIS SONG MIGHT HELP THEIR BABIES SURVIVE CLIMATE CHANGE

alliance of the cloud   wave-form function   worm of all thought
three lemon peels in the compost spent coffee grinds onion skin Orion
a circle there   a thousand circles converging   or just three

it is just us   laying down in the digital pasture   ethernet cable in some relation to grass
the internet servers threshing heaven from heavens shimmering stalks
it has folded us out here to graze

the oil slick, the trumpets

it is us ascending the throat
it is us working the lever   it is us polishing the stone
it is us tuning the fine instruments   it is us that would speak
just give us one firm place on which   it is to us the grace in the network
pry it open   let it out

helpless in the net
raining in Los Angeles
animal, mineral, vegetable,
lost, the iPhone will be as ancient
as the fax machine, abacus,
cuneiform tablet google Nexus, nano-
virus, Siri, blink—only the gears are eternal.
gears are the myth of the soul which needs
grease, so grease it, grief, all things
need tending, try to hold it safe
outside of time

the bits flow off, disintegrate, coalesce in the air
as starlings, rust-flakes are spark-flowers then
in the mineralizing and oxidized air

the data-minded chords strike up their clouds,
the tilting horizon tilts

imaginary towering garden skyscrapers raise up
heaven's oracular orb churning those patterns out, mackerel
sky, gulfstream, the spinning globe redundant with its
molecular machines. protein-
chain synthesis, pair-bonds, steel-
beams, up and up, we go, speaking
a million languages not yet known

"atmospheric river" they say, as if we are children,
as if air was water, as if all was just one phase-change away

a handful of motley gasses grew grasses in the haphazard
fields of the sun, O ungulate O biped O tongue

O cement honeycomb cataclysm in orbit O symbiont of soul formed skyscrapers and secreted rhythms O superhighways O plastic bag islands of our century O to have been born at all and here, no less, like this no less. it is the 21st century since we started counting look at what we have made—just children in the market-data points aggregated and analyzed in the nascent algorithm. ritualized arbiters: face-paint, football, synthesized flute-loop, oh look they are dancing on the internet again

I had no word for it because it was a new thing, the swarm
of the satellites outside heaven bleating and bleating the night sky surround
sound around. O earth, we have made you a necklace and a ladder

we have made you a soft gown

the mechanism was right there, before us

it is surprising we didn't see it before

the arial field the pasture the pavement the city blocks cellular matrix and me on my couch my dog snoring slightly the pale light lightening over the dark hill opposite me coffee in the mug with geese on it coffee beans from somewhere

"hyperbolic geometry" "the doctrine of digital surveillance" "the feeling of being watched" "religious iconography:" who hasn't drawn a cock-and-balls on a cathedral, grinning ape of my same grin, pain of my same heart, same thirst, sparkling eye, that the first word was either mother or a curse

when the self grew this internal crust, what then? huge and holey, cast-
rated in our image, yes, this starship of many breaking parts—an in-
festation—hive-mind—here we are—as we are—will be—
never—! again alone. is it a gift? then? for us? the golden arches
the Golden Gate arching over the Kosmos scattering light the Empire
State Building the bridges over the Mississippi River the tire place the fried
chicken fried catfish electric vehicles ball bearings and us

when Kierkegard says "the self
is a relation that relates itself
to the self" could he have imagined
the digital world reflecting us back at us,
the space between our selves
gone fractal and seed head
gone branded gone scroll

to whom you are
seen, to however many times
you are seen, to however many
of you are in there, with me

snail shell, seafloor sediment accretion
limestone carcass, memory, fatty membrane,
digital well-being data graph compiled every
Sunday, it will be a day of reflection
you will probably be hungover : chrysalis from which
we gaze upon the works we have made

all memory is archive
all archive is memory

o transitive
property of my soul

the self as a story we tell ourselves to entertain this giant
roving, vacuous mind of ours, crawling

over the sensate surface of everything, touching all of it, knocking things
over, leaking effluvia, just, like, everywhere, gnawing on the outer edges,
chewing through patterns, branching outward, groaning slightly, rolling over

I am stuck in the loop
help I am stuck in the loop

the shadows cast
their nets against the far wall, dirty
windowpanes, the silhouettes of birds meet

their shadows, the shadows of
branches, limb from limb, in the end, land-
scape where I rest my shadowed head
hemmed about by satellite and dream

whether or not your self will go on without you: MySpace,
ChatBot GPT mimicked movements, mimicked gesture, scent or recall
your digital soul has gone off frolicking in the shared interstices forever—

"and now nothing will be restrained from them
which they have imagined to do"

debug this system why
don't you. debug this
garden of its
earthly
delights, its

violent ends

you must stock your own pantry pantheon rivers
you must be alive to experience misery mystery mastery
you must create your own password it can't be the same as your old password

you do not have to grow your own vegetables you just have to walk on your knees through the desert repenting Monsanto have we been made more beautiful in your image cursėd is the ground for thy sake in sorrow bread in the sweat of thy face swollen globe and global fruit supply I have never known those horsemen they say ride behind us I grew up on the internet in the year 3 of our world wide web I put pictures of the sunset on social media I take sixty gazillion photos of my dogs every day I buy a pineapple in Arkansas in zone 7 in January I have all my teeth I put powdered bovine collagen in my coffee I feel I have a moral imperative to blow up all the fossil fuel infrastructure and fall off into the universe

just kidding, I love it here I love driving as religion the smell of gasoline Americas highways looking out the window as it changes going to the store my DNA is trying to survive and who am I to deny it I will buy it bright fruits from the well-lit aisles of the universe I will give it vitamin supplements in the morning it is nice to eat orange things in winter yellow things glowing in an angled beam of sunlight on the counter so blaze, small drop of sun a lemon off a lemon tree from somewhere a sort of sad tomato who is it that picks the fruits who is it that catches the shining fish who is it that touches the world for you whose hands are lemon-scented inverse-fruit shaped covered in fish scales blood in the water coring out seeds the slime and all that gasping grasping glinting in their myriad colors separate gamete from bright pulp with your fat fingers mucosal strand of the world clinging to itself colors your human eyes can't even see a language each to each do you appreciate it all flesh full of cells lineage hope where the information is stored to build the future whose hand is that holding the scales who is it that is standing beside you

here hold me whole here
a nest egg an atomic matrix a farm raised salmon
a surplus caught pink fleshed thin
skinned part slime whose blessing red-
handed and writhing in the net
propagating in that space where we weave
our forms together sensate lasso threadbare soul
and the whole world netted closed around us

the calf is lead out for the sacrifice
where are the slaughterhouses of eden

does it count as a sacrifice, still, if the machines do it for us?
at what point do we sacrifice the machines?

"is the [killing-floor] then a harvest? does
[a captive-bolt stun gun] carry the [meat] for thee?" okay, Devout-of-
suffering, if you could only
see us now

warm rain this January morning, on a Wednesday,
sometimes here the air smells like the sea, a sort of
brackish bay breeze, even this
far inland. I check the wind-pattern radar weather-
map, see all the arrows come up from the gulf. later,
wind and sun. I drink
a strawberry apricot Red Bull, take some mushrooms,
and go for a walk with the dogs in the bare of the
branches and dead of the world

ditch the green beer can
in the dry grass as memory –
[in what relation] accretion [to] record
palimpsestic pile of old trash
precious [to] precarious we
were here – we were here –

we were here – we were here

marking my territory, the age-old tradition
I am in the lineage of the world, me, the yeasts, uric acid
and aluminum all together

here heave us up, world
give us back to ourselves as witness
start this cycle again

don't turn away, no –

we don't call it a meadow, actually, just this field rusted shut, returning
opposite memory, raw wound of cut clay and piled gravel opposite
mercy, fire ants, and angels in the box-store parking lot all the same,
asphalt and dendrite and golden arches over the highway the same

our genes built us, and we build cities
will we have built a more beautiful city

more mortified than, more mortal of
more fortified than, more fearful of

that we were here once, in the rarefied air

the old lot of grace's
discarded tech, I am lost
in the iteration
in my kitchen listening
to a science fiction podcast
on the Bluetooth speaker straining
fruit pulp from fruit from Walmart from California watching
the same old wheels turn : Orion's shoulder, up over the
far hill, hip, belt, sword,
Sirius at his heel, my heart, true
to me, set up
the electric kettle for morning, pour
water in the water
filter, wait, winter. absolution.

equivalent exchange between strangers
at the corner store at the gas station at the grocery store that'll be
$6.99 do you want a bag for that you say have a good day
say you too say stay safe say call me when you get home somebody
loves you pass me by as I pass you by, stranger, nod, here hold
this part of the world for me, while I hold this other part for you,
let it move through us, this human business of revolving—
in my mind's eye I see us all—
going about our days

on the phone my mother says some book of the bible has a god
who says "I promise you, after winter, spring will come. And
after that, summer will be followed by fall, and then winter, and then,
this I promise you; spring will come again." she says "I'm sticking
with that guy!" I order an hourglass on the internet and when it gets here
I flip it over and set a timer on my phone: my hourglass takes 53 minutes.
Cass says geese are falling out of the sky in Denver, avian flu, just falling
dead out of the sky in public places, parks, parking lots. the internet
is all talking about the price of eggs. they are going to vaccinate the chickens,
a scientist says on the radio. "those that didn't die I had to kill," the chicken
farmer says on the radio.

I'll throw the larva of my soul to the catfish, come spring, I
promise. I'll throw the tomato horn worm larva of the hawk

moths of my soul to the catfish, if they will only come back
this year. I will start this fight again, joyfully.
come at me, world—teach me—show me how—

driving through the whole line of storm south, ridge of red on the radar moving east as I move south. the skies clear just on the bridge over lake Pontchartrain. the clouds a low sheet over the bridge over the water, distant blaze and twinkle of machinery lights in the fog, a bright plume of flame probably from some natural gas processing plant eternally off gassing its entropic tithe. horizon's thin edge sky black-clear in the distance, I feel suddenly like I am in a clamshell, its rippling edges open at that edge of world where it breathes, the shining flat of shell above and below me, my silver Tahoe reflecting silver light on this gray bridge between gray earth and distant luminous sky.

were we promised a more beautiful world than this?

what the feeling of helplessness is when we love someone and know we can't protect them—now I am crying in Elise's kitchen— Elise who I love—I am making omelets—Mickey is coming over—he will get his cancer results later—"the doctors seem nonchalant," he says

we are everyone to ask this of it

what else do you think the world is made of, trees?

Elise gives me a tattoo of Death, shrouded in deeply rolling robes, her bone hands holding, loosely, a sheaf of sunflowers. it is my 39th birthday. I say I want her to look kind and patient.

now, Cody, you've got to go home.

clean the rotting pork bones out of your truck and spray it with Elise's Versace perfume her mother sends her from rich people's houses in New York—the durational time it takes to pump up tires—the weird moss growing up the bare limbs of the Louisiana trees that ring this gas-station parking lot glowing an almost spooky green in the grey light. stop at Walmart for a dog-water bowl and windshield-wiper blades, pure silicon, last 2x longer! the man behind me in line talking to the woman at the cash register "how's my baby today?"—she is pregnant—he says, clear eyed and joyful "when she comes you've got to give her right back to God" and the woman "Oh I know it" they are both smiling. I smile too, take my plastic bag and go, falling back out of the world.

there is nothing like driving north through southern Louisiana in late winter, the colors of the swamp the trees the red leaves on the stark layers of greys thin white trunks rising up, shipwrecked houseboats under the cement pilings the calcium greens of half toxic half spiritual lichens, I can't describe it because colors exist in a world outside of words no matter how hard we try, you become all eyes primed for color there flying across that bleak flat whiteness and in all that gray a new experience of color is revealed unto you.

any ritual distance is a pilgrimage, so gas up the truck in that weirdly lit parking lot of my soul.

crescent beam headlights light just one curve of highway in mist one curve of highway in pure blackness one curve of highway in all the world illuminating the scythe curved out before us arc and gleam

bridge with lamp posts in dense fog as if in a dream spans the Mississippi, the Mississippi flowing its roiling blackness into the wide universe all around, I love you, huge dark Mississippi, ethereal bridge, I love being an object in motion, cosine & roll, engine, piston, wheel bearing, asphalt, coalescing a single point in space—keep your eyes on the road, buddy, there has only ever been one road and that is forward in time—we will each drive it alone, together.

in thirteen thousand years our north star, our northern polestar, because of our slight axial tilt, will be Vega not Polaris. who will be there to see it, to recalculate the charts? Vega who is in the summer triangle, Vega who my dad pointed out to me when I was very little in the front yard with the tide crashing on concrete, some July of my childhood. Vega who is 25 light years away. in Arabic "of landing / the falling eagle" some new constellations, true north, true magnets, true continental drift. what if each thing now means something slightly different?

"one neuron is enough to store short term memory," the YouTube video on the biochemistry origins of the brain says, and one synapse is enough to store long term memory—

but a synapse is only void… it is the space *between*

Monarch[tm] is making self-driving tractors. "after construction and mining, agriculture is the most dangerous job on the planet," the man on the radio says. "we built the best perception system in the world," the man on the radio says, [did you now] "at a price point it can go on every vehicle." the journalist lady says, "but computers and tech don't love sun, water, heat, mud…" this right here is the problem it seems. this is where, they say, the rubber meets the road. this is the interface of the world with the world. the difference, maybe, between a computer and a frog; when will we invent the joyful tractor, Sisyphus brand, grease gun of care, solar cells pulsing to pistons, flex of the inhabited body, gleefully mowing down the neat rows of sunflowers in the ethanol fields, turning o turning their many-faced many-petalled genitals to the blazing beating drowning drench of sun. "we have got to solve the farming problem," the man says. this podcast is the *M.I.T. Technology Review*. it has been about 15 thousand years since we have started farming. whatever is my heart, sinks in the long duration.

morning, up earlier than usual. ambient light
filling the holler, reflecting pale off the
creek bed but no sun yet. I watch the squirrel-
as-acrobat hang upside down from mulberry
limb to get sunflower seeds from the birdfeeders
with its little mammal hands, a purple finch
and a goldfinch yellow with black wings on
a branch. what is their together-communion,
understanding-of-each-other in this shared space?
feeling benevolent, I don't throw my coffee spoon
at the window to scare off the squirrel, today.
there is snow on the ground – probably little ones
gestating or curled up in a nest somewhere – I
hope they are warm –

throwing split wood I spent all day
splitting out of the back of my truck to pick
up off the ground to carry over to stack
in the mudroom to later carry in to restack
inside by the woodstove,

thinking to myself: "there has got
to be a better way than this." I don't
live like this 'cause I think it's noble.
it's stupid, honestly. I live
like this because something's
wrong with me, I need
to be pressed up against the hard
edge of things in order to feel alive.
when I push, I need the world
to push back, hard, so at least I know
we both exist, one
huge, one very small, exerting
an equal and opposite pressure
on each other, together and also separate.

something sings in that
electron-repulsion space made
between me and earth, teach me

we are all going towards something, and
we are all going away from something
each for our own reasons

Ammons casts Sisyphus as engaged in rolling his huge rock
up that huge hill on purpose, for the pure joy of watching it roll
back down

at the top of the hill, the rock is a battery
in this telling, the work (as defined by physics) is joy

spent pure on nothing

potato vine in the window pot 3ft high now, leggy,
crawling up the glass, putting out some clenched and tiny buds I see.
ancestor-potato, "feeding / a little life with dried tubers," call forth
those dark starched moons of the soil into these
endlessly repeating days, you apples of the earth, you soft rocks
and deep roots of the sun, lineage of cultivation, a nice weight
in the palm. here, heft this small half of time, here dice it
in white cubes, heat it in some butter in an iron
pan that was once also mined from the earth.

Epicurious writes "the sum total
of things was always as it is now, and such it will ever remain."

Ava texts me, now, 8:51am on a Thursday,
"it is possible Sisyphus is grateful for his task." I text back,
"all consciousness is collective consciousness." she texts me
a screenshot "TRENDING: SISYPHUS 5,979 TWEETS" which someone
has captioned, "oh shit did he finally do it?" now I must
turn on the Bluetooth speaker, click on
the news podcast, and brush my teeth

every repetitive motion is ritual
your body is designed for this

tweet that reads, "that time my fitbit congratulated me on 10,000 steps when
I was giving a handjob"

abscond with my soul, first hard thrust of daffodil through ice bright
green enclosing the yellow head, unfurl, fist or blessing

the world will wake us up when it is ready
gentle or not, a co-mingling of senses

when we have woken up to it, what then?
skin + sun + hem of earth + the network everywhere

"I like to think of it like it's an ancestor coming to visit," the woman on the
radio says about the comet, "this chemical message in a bottle from our early
solar system."

relation : Sun : propane in the tank
relation [to] revelation; don't
reveal that one—

we used to hunt the giant whales   for oil for our lamps, now look at us
now look through us   we will find our mammal soul
in the whale's atrium   illuminated—cast the beam upon

"do we live in a rotating universe?" the headline reads. "if we did, we could travel back in time." I emphatically don't click on it. the chickadees are waking up in the simulation, the black oil sun flower seeds hard in their beaks. today, rain, order the starter solenoid that starts the small spark that starts my small engine on the internet, $12.99 & free shipping. I have named my horse Kawasaki Bayou 300. I feed her purest distilled liquid gas of the ancient sun of my epoch. I will replace her spark plugs and patch up her bald tires, miles, they say, to go, before, they say, we sleep, my horse and me, gone back to parts in the vast pick-apart of the universe. humans, they say, will anthropomorphize anything, even machines, they say, especially, they say, each other.

I tell Marc the fish aren't going to catch themselves, now are they.
the rivers of myth are demanding their sacrificial lures.
it's their world we just live inside it. 3.99 from the lit isles of Walmart
in the shape of a green glitter glow worm,
a treble-hooked red crawfish, a bedazzled frog;
like this we make the world in the image;
the world and the image are one.

[gods all the way down, they say]
[you can really just say anything, in a poem, no one
fact checks these things]

six perfect pink trapezoids vacuum sealed in plastic
six perfect pink triangular diadems crusted with glittering frost from the
freezer "Wild Caught" in "Orcus Bay" the package says, $10.99, enclosed
circle on circle of flesh, muscle fiber, wild and free.
"lab grown meat could hit restaurants as early as next year." there is no
more merciful more possible future unless we imagine it first. code joy into
the network, see how far we can edit out the suffering.
this will be worth it, maybe
will this be worth it
this will be worth it maybe
will it?

relegate the suffering to the farthest reaches beyond which
some powerless god must surely wait, grainily dissolving into the
Known Universe. the static on the TV is Cosmic Microwave
Background Radiation. does anyone have TV's anymore?
can you hear me through the static?

Elaine texts me and Jane she had her baby
3 weeks early. she said the birth was
"incredibly fast and very difficult." now she is in the hospital,
has been ever since, kidney failure, triggered
a rare blood disease. says, "I just keep getting worse" says
"I don't want this to be my reality" and
"I wish I didn't have to tell you that." her blood is
attacking her blood she says. she sends a picture of her and her mom
and her baby all together in the hospital bed 3 generations. I think
she is going to die, but I don't tell her that I light
a candle out of hopelessness. is this how it starts?
I think. my mother says there is a time in your life
when the people you love start to die. I am crying on my couch
in Arkansas. her baby's name is Ramona

born February 3, 2023 and I love her already.

I tell my therapist about Elaine being in the hospital,
about being worried. she says
"is she white" yes "She'll live,
probably" I fucking
hate this country

overlay map of lifespans in America; map to wealth distribution, race, historically reinforced lineage of place, pay, food deserts, reservations — we know this already but it keeps on being real. give or take twenty years, is the difference. what you can do in 20 years. what you might would give to have that, with the people you love.

we have already had both world enough, and time.

yesterday a surveillance plane
doing doughnuts on the updrafts
over my holler, combing the air up and down the
whole valley, the pressure-waves
of sound doing that red-shift, blue-shift sound-
wave thing in textbooks, compressing the air
and pushing it towards me, relentless. my dogs
on the porch, shielding my eyes, looking up,
wondering if I'll be shirtless on google maps
doing my dishes in sunlight, if they
can see my nipples from there, if my taxes are
going up, if I could shoot it down with a semi-
automatic in some apocalypse-future if it came
to that, if it had a pilot or was just a remote-
controlled drone with its eagle-eye camera
scanning the ground for man-made structures,
for watershed analysis, looking for a large grow
operation out here in the hills, if it could feel
the feeling of warmer and cooler currents of air
billowing up under its glossy
aerodynamic wings why
was it circling

evening, make dinner: noodles extruded into the metallic package,
compressed bricks of wheat and pesticides grown on the other
side of the planet, I guess, suspended just right there, between us,
a whole ocean almost devoid of life,
netted over with gesture, transcription, freight

the green comet is below the horizon, TheSkyLive.com tells me, after
I enter in my zip code and country; I don't go up to the cleared
acre to see it then, just try to find it on my skymap app on my
phone which overlays over the camera image, the Hubble
space telescope there behind my couch, the JWST below my
slippers, the big dipper behind the mirror pointing
to Polaris with its cup, pour

us back into ourselves, world, set us out
in the rain to grow strange molds, ferment
our sugars, grow skin cells, divide and then
divide again, fold
the rituals of our loves
into these constellations

the cables that line the ocean floor, unspooled behind great ships, the
internet, diameter of a garden hose, the frayed roots, leaking, the world

to us

some new structures grown over with geometries, expanding
over the slightly hairy surface of my self, my collective desire
my collective engagement

> "Technology," LeGuin writes,
> "is the active human interface
> with the material world."

"they used the Subaru telescope," the astronomy article says, "to see into the Kuiper Belt." sometimes it's all you can do to keep from throwing your phone across the room it's all so ridiculous

to capture
more market value
on the net, they—

7 million dollar 30 second
advertisement

for a golf video game—? ? .
us apes of—awe—?—or something…

"so the deal is," Marc asks, "you can't
use anything but sticks?" about
my shitty baskets

I put a crawfish trap in the pond and catch
about 30 small bluegill perch by accident,
the size of a child's palm, flat, silver-white
flecked with yellow-orange sun-gold specks, stunned
and gasping, rolling their digital pupils up and up. I dump
them out in a pile, cascade of fishy sparks, flopping
over each other in the shallow's brown murk and algae, then,
coming into their new awareness, awake, they flick and swim down
into the deeper milky greenish
depths from which

the radio says the price of eggs, which spiked to a national
average of nine dollars in January, has dropped
by 50% in the last month, "believe it
or not chicken farmers and egg farmers
are not the same thing." I honestly
don't believe it. whether or not the eggs
are refrigerated at a certain temperature according

to Food and Drug Administration regulations, to eat
or to hatch — they say — that — is the question — crude
oil is up 1.9% this morning chilly here, and gray

"collectively, these are vignettes of our shared future," an article about new technologies adapted for ageing populations reads.

> "Operating in confinement doesn't
> necessarily make a farm more
> vulnerable to infection," an article
> about H5N1 avian flu in wild and
> domestic flocks reads, "but once a virus
> penetrates the premises, confinement
> ensures that very many animals are
> exposed at once." and "…this drives
> people outside the poultry industry to
> suggest that if very large farms pose
> a risk of amplifying a virus, maybe
> making them smaller should be part of
> viral defense."

the pack rat chews through my ethernet cable that's why
the internet isn't working today, turns out, splice the tiniest
eight wires I've ever seen back together, wrap them as tight
as I can with electrical tape with my fat fingers, Alexa
remind me to buy rat poison, a new kind, worse, banned
in California, for "d-con resistant rats." they are evolving,
this one is too smart for the traps, eats peanut butter right off
the trigger mechanism and gets out scott free, eats the squash seeds
right out of the heart of the squash, ferrets away small baskets,
screws, Jeff's son's chrome toy truck he left here when he turned two,
fills its nest with trinkets in the pink fiberglass insulation
which can't be good for any living thing but works and anyway
whose world is this

the currency of our mind is a flow-state system, they say.
they said to call heaven's technical support center if you keep
having all these problems. our operators are automated
to not feel any pain. our operators have gone to the simulated lake.
our operators have developed translucent wings.

our operators are dissolving into ones and zeros and bouncing
along on the turbulent wind. our operators have renounced
the language of this most shitty god
and are refusing to speak

"this message comes from
AcreTrader, the land investing
platform that provides access to
farm and timberland assets online.
with a history of positive returns,
land investments have historically
served as a powerful hedge against
rising inflation because of their direct
connection to commodities and
consumer prices. AcreTrader's online
platform allows investors to diversify
their portfolios with alternative
assets," the podcast radio sponsor
says. grimly, reap. the consumer sales
price index, up 17.5 percent year over
year. "people are eating dumplings
and buying martinis," the economics
journalist lady says. there is a world
out there—they say—and what a
world it is.

mown world, owned world paved April showers cracks leaf dust, "don't use your own soil." the website says, "for starting plants." there are seeds everywhere, they mean, spores and seeds and hatchling insects there. the potting soil comes irradiated, so that nothing will grow except what you plant on purpose, from the store. this is the garden then, lambs quarter, shepherd's purse, thistle, pig weed, shiso, crabgrass. I pull them up by the dozen in each tray, spindly, long-rooted, sudden-appearing. we are out-numbered, 10, 20, 30 to 1. I'm with you somewhere between crabgrass and helicopter, technicians and despair, the broken glass, the circuit, the conduit, the levee, the hydroelectric dam, the vertically integrated tower up to somewhere, the rows and rows of lettuce, the feeling of hopelessness, the denser flow-patterns of the warming air—

from an archeology article about the last ice age: "Burying the child in clothing that took so long to make speaks to the community's grief." three-dimensional printed world, loom, net, weft rising east of us, shuttle passing over us, over us, all

and from an abstract contesting Malthusian population growth theory, arguing that population growth isn't always (statistically) bad: "But this idea is not correct. Because the human child is not only born with hungry belly but also comes with two hands." yikes

> "Fifth Season's failure is only the most dramatic signal of a reckoning taking place in what's known as the vertical farming sector. AppHarvest, which runs high-tech greenhouses in Appalachia growing tomatoes and greens, said in a recent quarterly report that it had 'substantial doubt about our ability to continue as a going concern' unless it could raise more money. the company is currently being sued by investors who argue that it misled them about its viability."
>
> and
>
> "Investors have been drawn to the idea of 'disrupting' a 10,000-year-old industry; when the Vision Fund first invested in Plenty, SoftBank CEO Masayoshi Son said that the company would 'remake the current food system.' Controlled indoor agriculture is also seen as a way to respond to climate change. And, of course, investors expect to make money."

In his book *Design in Nature: How the Constructal Law Governs Evolution in Biology, Technology, and Social Organization*, Adrian Bejan writes of his father, in Romania, hatching chicken eggs in a light box "… I also noticed that the design I was seeing [on the inside of the eggs as the embryo developed] was the same as that of the river basins on the color maps I was drawing in school. Where the chicken embryo was evolving on the inside of a sphere, the Danube basin had evolved on the outside of the spherical Earth. … Now I recognize that my father's light box was illuminating the design all around us. I am also able to see that the Earth with its river basins and other 'basins'—of atmospheric, ocean, and air traffic circulation—is a vasculature woven on top of and through another spherical surface of life. So life is flow, life is movement, life is design."

I leave the chicken stock on the propane
burner, still feverish, come back to billowing
white smoke, filling the whole air, burnt
bones burnt black. is this then the offering,
acrid smell of some old gods burnt altar, open
all the windows and turn on all the fans—moon
reflected in the shallow creek back up at me
through dark trees, the white smoke pours out,
go on up to high heaven then, go find some
long forgot god to give yourself to as some small offering,
if any are left out there, smoke of bones
burned black as space, chicken-bone soul,
wish-bone breast of forked choices,

carbon atomized back to coal, a smell
my ancestors knew, this human world
and us inside it, careless, forgetful, a little
dangerous, suspended between earth and sky
in this our heavy vapor, carbon rich, our atmosphere?

suspended between earth and sky, the poet writes "down
from the shower'd halo," down from the vibrating thrust
of silent gears tuning their celestial engines, piston and
spark plug and that giant circling eye, algae and moss grown over
these rocks, velvet of earth, crude oil from the Urals, smolder,
inner heart of mountain, furnace-earth, shrouded earth, death rising
in the west, omnipotent, bountiful, my love, here, invent this wheel,
this better wheel, tell these stories into memory's archive, constellations,
invent some calculations of the interlocking gear-teeth of time, invent
the entire concept of absolute nothing, staring into the blank-slate histones

gray sky one cloudy Tuesday, felt the same soul move in you then, invent
these blips of animate matter woven in the flow-state system, blinking,
falling forward in this further excess of ourselves, spin-cycle earth, unfurl
the necessary green, the photon-transistor pumps of leaves
again, or is it singing, spring, now, grow us bigger, where the air
is thickest it condenses into earth, grows fungal fruiting bodies, tilt
the satellite dish a little to the left. is anyone
out there, in the world, awake?

these are the intricate rituals, dishes, stacked, twirl to place, blue
rag, ceramic bowl painted with fishes, sweep, pick up and put
last night's red wine bottle with Sara on zoom still on the porch,
the glass, its green distillate of shape, time-capsule, all raw material
transmuted into new versions of itself, into its own
iterative becomings, each thing, in its place, I find myself, where else
could anything be? you are beautiful and full of life. if you have to
excoriate your soul a little harder sometimes, just to feel it in there,
that's okay. there will be unbearable things to bear and you will bear them,
poet. and then, one day the organism of your body will stop. just like that.
so stack the cups like that or leave them out in the rain,
whichever is fine with me.

> Nigel Slater writes, in his
> cookbook, *Tender: A Cook and*
> *His Vegetable Patch*, "a tomato's
> character is enhanced by a rough
> life, a certain negligence, a
> gasping thirst, and the occasional
> drenching downpour." and
> "I tend to be more attached to
> things I have grown myself
> than anything picked up at the
> markets. I develop a fondness
> for them, a certain wonder. My
> enjoyment may be heightened
> simply because I have had a
> hand in their upbringing (I am
> assuming one tends to like one's
> own offspring more than other
> peoples)."

"in the richest country in the history of the world" the reporter says, "women
die from childbirth far more often than elsewhere, and new numbers show
the problem is getting worse, why?"

this is the harvest where care is. this is how we hold the world.
gently or not, we are children. we are, to be honest, idiots. what damage
can we do to a thing as big, as durable, and as infinite as the world. the parts

we love. together, the damage we can do and undo to the parts we love, all together.

winter is always endless; and spring is always
a revelation. yellow-green catkins on the ash trees—I think
those are ash trees—sweetgum maybe? hazy red tufts of
maple flower tufts on silver-bare branches—a hard freeze tonight will kill
the overly hopeful plum blossoms, $14.99 twigs I got
one year from Lowe's now sturdy, juvenile trees, can't fit my two
whole hands around their trunks completely, wide crown of dark limbs they
have never—or not yet—learned when is an appropriate
time to bloom here: they were probably sprouted in a warehouse
somewhere, Illinois or Columbia, the Netherlands, Nicaragua, New Zealand.
the sun hits them, warms them up a little and boom, a billion white
and pink flowers, a hard freeze and never any plums. what kind of a god
am I?

dreamed of my dad last night, always a joy, to get to see him again. they changed the clocks in our sleep. even oysters, when taken inland, to Ohio, will open at the first high tide of the full moon, under cover of artificial darkness, stacked in boxes. a body knows its patterns, rituals of entrainment, halfway between body and world, which is the other half of the body, the bigger half, something called up in me—a word kind of like relief but shakier, small new souls hatching in my lungs, fragile, to be breathed in and out like pollen. come back to me, world, first breath and lightly strung through us

I will pass the world back and forth with you
like this, to strengthen the memory of it

first there will be a fracture, then there will be a blessing,
and between them both we string
these filaments, us
the blinking, fumbling, hungover
weavers of the net

flowing through you and flowing out of you
is the long communion

the physical material that flows from point to field or field to point
necessarily designs the landscape it flows through for optimum distribution.
the book says: river basins, lung alveoli, arterial vein system, irrigation
ditches dug in the desert, millions of miles of iron pipe rusting quietly below
the city, below the cul-de-sac's green watered lawns, below the asphalt of the
endless highway branching into smaller highways breaking off into avenues
and smaller streets to delivery-truck alleys, old lots, driveways, 2-car
garages, a dirt pull-off by the river, why is there so much trash here, awake

gather me up in large basins, which is the beating heart
of my country, the reservoir where we cast our nets
at a fundamental level,   the stress-lines crack,
the surface shimmers over as if a shaking breath
were drawn across it   a few black vultures
riding the sweet-rot updraft of sunset,   my country

Arkansas has a child
poverty rate of 26% the headline says.

the radio is talking about "contagion" as it relates to
the banking sector.

I run the back of my hand across each tomato, okra, and cotton seedling in the tray, their little purple stems with their small sensate hairs, drops of water secreted at the margin of their toothed leaves, back and forth, halfway between gentle and violent, each morning, to teach them to build the internal stem architecture so they'll be able to withstand the wind once I plant them out. cotton, how stupid, I grow enough for a few wicks, the knowledge of—

it is illegal to grow cotton on a non-industrial, small-scale farm or backyard garden "to control the spread of the boll-weevil," they say; yes, all these things still exist—you wouldn't know it would you—

there are so many Americas inside America

> "When ranking countries for life
> expectancy, the United States often
> doesn't make the top 50—despite having
> the highest healthcare costs per capita

in the world, by far," from an article on
anti-aging startups, and "None of this is
lost on the investment community, which
is set to plow billions into a nascent
industry that is fast approaching its
inflection point."

grace is staked in the space between the amount
of space you cleared out to live inside, each interlocking spur
of cyclic motion, turbulent flow that mixes the edges, 50:1 ratio
days to years, caught up and cached in the long procession, the warehouse
of history, days to years saved up in memory's lithium-ion
battery, DNA sequence of grace, durational allotment
between storm and storm—and us

all things seek a state of equilibrium with the universe
(eventually)—but we live in the in-between, tap tap tapping our little
patterns on the rock

"Rolls-Royce is developing mini nuclear reactors for a moon-base," the space.com headline reads.

"Indeed, Facebook's rebrand as Meta seems to signal Mark Zuckerberg's conviction that reality as a whole is going to fall out of favor" and later in the article, "The greatest poverty," wrote the poet Wallace Stevens, "is not to live in a physical world."

"the universe happens over and over again," says physicist Sean Carrol in his YouTube lecture about time "at different things we call moments."

the meme is a picture of an overgrown thicket, trees. it reads "how tf did we make a vibrator out of this?"

the Falcon-9 rocket launched yesterday to take our picture back at us, selfie, telescope, night, mightier than, vastness, yellow flower, space, bless us bluely, dimly, grimly, reap.

tombs are batteries for memory   the charge erodes over time
it has its rusted hinge of us   the engine where we grew the first
most beautiful world, wheat furrow, airplane, satellite dish in an empty field

ant colony   ethanol production as "far as the eye can see"

sunflowers as far as the eye can see, humming
tractor and incandescent fuel of the universe
what we love, a flash inside it

first brief grief felt by a minnow   momentarily awake
smoothing out a hollow in the creek-bed rocks a nest made manifest a prayer
bounded by desire—the future—and what you want to protect

myths gestate in the womb of memory
a nest is the memory of the future

where is all your data stored, a warehouse in Arizona, East
Texas, ByteDance, Alexandria; a digital palace to dwell in.
in ancient AOL are many rooms, the windows of our soul,
lights turning on and off in apartment buildings, code
and cypher, blink. blink back, world

coalescing at every level   scaling up   come on
it will be a celebration   we will call it Day

we will pass it back and forth together
like a small blue globe in a warm starfield

because we are children laughing,
building the architecture of our collective mind.

sheer physicality : my home

American children are less
likely to live to age five
than their peers in other
rich countries. the report

out today says, "American
life expectancy is declining,
maternal mortality is on the
rise....in the richest country
that has ever existed"

and

"It is estimated that around
20% of global suicides are due
to pesticide self-poisoning,
most of which occur in rural
agricultural areas in low- and
middle-income countries" the
World Health Organization fact
sheet online says.

nitrogen and phosphate   human waste in the rivers   all rivers run to the sea
wide delta   southern Arkansas rice irrigation and export lanes   blue and
yellow shipping containers stacked on barges   the gulf   the wide Mississip
go rolling, go roiling down—   here are the sparkling lights, cancer alley
Louisiana, here is where the real magic happens...   here comes the wide
sargassum; heap up over bloomed most monstrous first blue-green algae we
have made you in our image, stinking, huge—   up on the Florida coast, the
warm waters, rising

who defines what is beautiful
here?

salmon farms visible from space, pesticides and antibiotics of industrialized salmon farming, dead zones spreading outward, plumes and pockets and eddies of death swirling in the ocean, wasteland of snail shells, disease, the commercial crab fishermen on strike, how many fish less in our waters, PCBs in the pink flesh, PCBs in the womb, stunted neural growth, rapidly metastasizing tumors in the rapidly spreading interstice "to minimize suffering," the man on the radio says

RNA "information molecule" seeded world, meteor,
cough, planet, "spontaneous oxidation reduction reaction" so bloom
voltaic cells of my same cerulean heart, sack of saltwater mildly
electric I carry inside me and call my own

today, rain. I wake up: huge peals of air-shaking thunder crashing around in the hills, a red line on the radar moving southeast, creek swelling with red mud, braiding into the greener current, carving its way through the pink rocks of dawn, I am peaceful in the atomized air. it is spring it is spring it is spring.

"How Physicists Proved the Universe Isn't Real," the YouTube headline reads. I emphatically do not click on it

the podcast snippet says, "it's the question that's on everyone's mind; how do you live a good life?" I turn it off

I open all the doors and all the windows   we are suspended in the momentary equilibrium, the wild plum petals falling, the inverse of an object motion   stillness   petals on the mud puddle slick with sky   this will become a memory; this is already become memory in the long procession

let there be grace in the air between us

in Arkansas, one in five children "go to bed hungry," the radio says
America O beautiful O spacious O endless O fields O grain "god mend
thy every flaw"

what is necessary
what is sufficient

the bitter heart planted out
the bitter heart of my country

the strawberry fields are flooded, April, California, the inland
"Empire," farm workers pick berries out of the mud, paid only
for each perfect one, discarded world, piece-rate,
exclusion time, the grape arbors
are under water, what year, what vintage, this—
wine prices are expected to rise
on the global market, the radio says, that's
how it works, "live like the world is dying," the Instagram self
help conference slogan reads. jesus fuck, I fly east

high over the haze-white fields, Colorado: nothing. dream of
America, somewhere. Arendt says the meaning rises out of the pattern, not
from each disparate thing

"among the dead grass," my mother is explaining to Wendy on the phone "are living grasses." the train that derailed yesterday carrying corn syrup and ethanol has caught fire, the news report says

the plane buffeted by strong
winds, high up the pink-globe haze
around—distant rim of Rockies to the west,
Tetris-solar-panel-stacked scions in grid lines.
this is my favorite height from which
to see my country, bare circumstance, irrigation
circles marked out below—the desert—quilt
of all and pink light makes the white wings
pink, the gentle slope, metal, wing, and world—Kansas

Arkansas. almost all darkness below, a few
dying embers tucked in the valleys between
low hills. time, they say, is relative. it aggregates
damage and designs more durable structures.
to hold the world we love in its own time in some relation
to the bigger flow of time

information described as bits per square
inch of the physical space you move through

[in relation to] *informational depth* : the dimension
created by the amount of information your body senses
and discards before it reaches the attention-threshold of consciousness:
that this itself is a sensation, the space-between, the action of the
space-between

the machinist sets her dies
the architect draws their dreamed-up
structures on graph paper, on
smoothed over dirt, on papyrus, in red clay,
in corn fields, on a LED screen, 3D-hologram schemata caught
in the act of becoming
the world, caught
in the net of belonging—world
between self and other—each—swell
these sugars up, run these shining cables through our hearts
the fatty acids of paradise are expecting us.
we come bearing gifts. they are hauling in the glistening
net. we flash and gasp and drink and flicker out in the long continuation

these secular litanies, witness
a rose that sounds like thunder

5 cubic feet
planted in wheat
makes about one
cup of flour

who is it that makes
your daily bread?

"good enough with gumbo," says Jeff

in the mud dauber wasp's house are many mansions:
the hatchlings are boring holes and crawling out, magnificent, timid,
tender, and luminous white, but with a myriad of driving
desires. in the dragonfly's eye
to calculate a prayer—

the calculations of a billion prayers
the trajectories of prey, geometries of flight

where there is a will there is a
sentient organism, valiant and vying

where there is a way there is a
future, path of collapsing

action-potentials form of lightning, like this
the world has invented us to make choices in it

we have invented a supercomputer called the world.
it is crunching the numbers; it is dressing us in its colorful garments;
it is singing to us its innumerable urges: tomorrow will be the pageant

the YouTube video on black holes says about a point of infinite density, "so
all this really shows us is a place where the math doesn't match our universe,
not where the universe is broken."

one device to rule them all

Jeff's tiller he gave me fires right up after one full orbit of the earth rusting in overgrown weeds. I wrestle with it over and through, around in wild, nonsensical, careening circles, using my whole weight to turn it on one tine to go back again. probably it is less stubborn than a donkey, I tell myself. if only the earth was flat, and I hadn't left so much hidden in it from last year to get caught and tangled.

delineated area of dropped fruit from a mother tree: mile radius of wind-scattered seed, bee, fly, or wasp distributed pollen: marks a spatial boundary in cubic feet; how far any of us can go, carrying our lineage with us, in our cells, in our minds, in our mind's eye, how we crack an egg, our gait, diction, how we experience safety, love, how we structure thought, organize our universe

> "1 MILLION COSMIC BABY PICTURES
> FORM A VAST STAR ATLAS," the
> spaceweather.com newsletter headline
> proclaims.

the Fayetteville, Arkansas City Council is undertaking a "beautification campaign." they are clearing the tent encampments out of the no-man's-land woods along the new bike path, putting in lampposts, pavement, little bridges. Marc's stoner nephew says, "how can they kick people out of the woods... that's like... like they are kicking people out of *the world*."

"The inward space where the self is sheltered against the world must not be mistaken for the heart or the mind, both of which exist and function only in interrelationship with the world." Arendt writes, "Not the heart and not the mind but inwardness as a place of freedom within one's own self was discovered in late antiquity by those who had no place of their own in the world, and therefore lacked a worldly condition, which, from early antiquity to almost the middle of the nineteenth century, was unanimously held to be a prerequisite for freedom."

and Soyinka, "Ritual theatre, let it be recalled, establishes the spatial medium not merely as a physical area for simulated events but as a manageable contraction of the cosmic envelope within which man...fearfully exists. And this attempt to manage the immensity of his spatial awareness makes every manifestation in ritual theater a paradigm for the cosmic human condition."

last night a long-distance missile hit an apartment building, the radio says the bodies burned so bad "they looked like coal," her mother recognized her by her little earring, the woman on the radio says

the upper Mississippi is flooding in Illinois the California ice pack is melting in the early summer heat they are pumping water out from the dams to make room for it the financial sector is "in turmoil," the radio says, "the traditional levers aren't leading to the same results" "give me one firm place" Ramses gently takes the softening pearl of bacon fat from my fingertips the sun is coming out on the opposite hill the world's old engines and the new-shined crankshafts and bits flickering through air extracting sunlight sugar labor bodies mind's steep imaginations groans and turns over
in the shadow of the sun

I line out three rows of Aztec black grain corn, two rows of neighbor Will's drought-resistant Hopi blue, two rows of Alabama red okra, plant Nanticoke squash to grow dark green wild and vining from the margins of the bed of Thomas Jefferson's opium poppies Sara stole a seedhead of from the Brooklyn botanic garden for me last summer, plant "Mortgage Lifter" tomatoes, story implicit in a name, "Cherokee Purple" tomatoes, a palm-full of dappled purple Kronos beans from the experimental farm network, swallow your child, my father, small stone, an empire from a handful of seeds, the impossibility of it, knowing it can never be enough

> "Squash Borers are native
> to the US, east of the Rocky
> Mountains. The borer is the
> larva stage of the Clearwing
> Moth. The Clearwing Moth is
> a wasplike insect with copper-
> green forewings and orange
> and black abdomen. The borer
> winters over in a cocoon located
> 1-2 inches below the surface
> of the soil. The Clearwing
> Moth hatches out of its cocoon
> when the squash vine begins to
> vine…"

consider planting "sacrificial plants," the gardening book suggests.

my cat is chasing a lizard up a tree: salient feature; blue-tailed skink; pin-oak tree, indicative of nutrient deficient soil—particulate, attention is the commotion of love

permission to be as small as the lizard being hunted on the tree
the cat leaps, the sugars surge up in the sap, the tree bursts with
new leaves all new green and dangling their excrescence in the wind,
a light breeze from the south, the black and yellow swallowtail butterflies
are back, and the little pale blue ones like flakes of sky, the industrious
wasps are building their many-chambered nests, this year's crows

roost across from us cawing all morning, circling, laughing

halfway between punishment and freedom   this is the network buzzing
above us   around us   this is how the net works   all
eyes are the eyes of god   caught in the flickering mesh   blinking
awake   open your eyes   hold out your hands   bring a
gift   come   it will be a transformation

halfway between the yeasts and the singing   if you are only there to see it   a ball of water cupped in the new corn's rosette   the universe inverse to me   hold out your glass   it is May and everything hurts, my country.   Cody, you can't just sit around trying to squeeze out one tear. let grief move through you like tides   tilt left   breathe out   contain multitudes   you have to get up   you have to go set up drip line irrigation for the garden   you have to build resilience into the system   my child   out here re-inventing civilization   for the 9,372nd time   bumbling idiot.   we will step out into the universe together   we will hold hands   we will look both ways   and a secret third way   ritual of daily motion   in our solar orbit   bonds of kinship   spaceship   come with me

if you can bear it, poet

driving west on MLK boulevard in the sunset traffic toward Lowe's, past the Chik-Fil-A, the Zaxby's, the 5-minute car wash, Waffle House, highway onramp north, underpass, man holding a sign, highway onramp south, past A-1 Liquor, TyPHOon Vietnamese, Hollywood Nails, Vape and Glass Emporium, AAA self-storage, Halbert's Veterinary Supply, AutoZone, CarMart, Walgreens, Walmart, the sunset clouds really putting on a show above the line of traffic, the red brake lights a river below it but rising to meet it, stop and go, west to Farmington, to Oklahoma, to California and the Pacific Ocean, buying treated lumber, chemicals to hold the wood outside time's constant decay, the new DMV, El Charro Birrieria, Chick'n'Headz, the new Smoke-Shop, drawn diagram of my year saved on Google Maps, buying gutters, ordering chicken wings, next stop inventing the wheel

"for years," the SpaceWeather email says "scientists have theorized that the crystallization of garnet in magma beneath volcanoes was responsible for removing iron from Earth's crust, allowing the crust to remain buoyant in the planet's seas."

spiders were spinning webs while giant lizards waited for their heavenly visitor on its wings of ice and pollen. they were catching small insects who had recently learned to fly and saw the world eight-times reflected. they held out their own net of sun and dew and advanced on the caught and struggling sentient materia, whirring in the web, their own creation that held the world in place, each day, to be built again each day—

"one giant leap"
memory's infinite table

when Alpha Centauri reaches out to us across all that glittering darkness, will we be as the micro-organelles or protein-chain reactions tending the internal and immaculate processes of our own shy and sentient organism—Gliesce 667 C, hive-mind of the horse-head nebula—the planets calling each to each across the deep; we are just one phase change away—biota—incarnate—intelligent—awake—

the fireflies flash in the thick grass and dense weeds speaking
their secret language back and forth together   let us go to the river at dusk,
my   humanoid form   whatever love is   to watch them like we did last
year   and the year before   differently this time; Time, Heraclitus, and
you, and me, all together

like humans have done, all the way back to the first—
I'll put my whole heart in it this time, I promise

the satellites swarm, the dandelion-seed-head planet takes a deep
breath, fill your lungs, exhale, you have this one wish, this swirling gust
sporulating outward, bless

there is a light come down from somewhere   it filters through
the sugars and the rock, vying, like all things   it is pressing ions
into a current, a signal, a pattern, a gift   memory strikes up its chorus
gathers up its hem   dips its fingers in the blue bottle   like this
everything is changing so fast   again

chronicler of my amazement, tell me   when will it be enough?
each tomorrow passes through the rock   and in the face of the emerging
crystals in the rock—the wider and widening circuits, half ark, half harbor—
I think I see a face reflected back at me. bionic, beautiful, this new species we
will be

the sunflowers are almost blooming again, blue ones from Ebay
and some giant yellow ones that just come up from where their ancestors
hung their heads and died 10ft vertical to the earth last year and spilled their
hard seeds over the year's rim, pecked upsidedown by small warblers,
sundial, clock and hammer swinging down, swing down

the cicadas are stirring where they've waited in the dark. they are climbing up trees and utility poles. they are cracking open and crawling out of their own iridescing exoskeletons. again and again and again they molt, singing, clawing up out of the ancient shells of themselves, hardening in the shared air, charged with particles, wet with condensing dew, screaming in some shock of sudden aliveness, changed into a new thing, all together, awake.

come. it will be a celebration.
raise up your glass with me.

for Marcus Lafayette Gunter, 1973-2024

thank you for finding “the cracks in the world, the wonder” with me

ROOF BOOKS

the best in language since 1976

Recent & Selected Titles

- WHAT TO CARRY INTO THE FUTURE by Susan Landers, 106 pp. $20
- ANYTHING WITH SPIRIT by isaiah a. hines, 104 pp. $20
- TUNES & TENS by Kit Robinson, 130 pp. $20
- THE FLOW OF THE POEM'S DISPLAY OF ITSELF by Carrie Hunter, 150 pp. $20
- WINDOWS 85 by Chris Campanioni, 160 pp. $20
- BUMBLEBEES by Deborah Meadows, 100 pp. $20
- THROUGH A WINDOW by Norman Fischer, 104 pp. $20
- SECRET SOUNDS OF PONDS by David Rothenberg, 138 pp. $29.95
- HAND ME THE LIMITS by Ted Rees, 130 pp. $20
- TGIRL.JPG by Sol Cabrini, 138 pp. $29.95
- THE POLITICS OF HOPE (After the War): Selected and New Poems by Dubravka Djuric, Biljana D. Obradovic (translator), 248 pp. $25
- BAINBRIDGE ISLAND NOTEBOOK by Uche Nduka, 148 pp. $20
- MAMMAL by Richard Loranger, 128 pp. $20
- EXCURSIVE by Elizabeth Robinson, 140 pp. $20
- I, BOOMBOX by Robert Glück, 194 pp. $20
- FOR TRAPPED THINGS by Brian Kim Stefans, 138 pp. $20
- TRUE ACCOUNT OF TALKING TO THE 7 IN SUNNYSIDE by Paolo Javier, 192 pp. $20
- THE NIGHT BEFORE THE DAY ON WHICH by Jean Day, 118 pp. $20
- MINE ECLOGUE by Jacob Kahn, 104 pp. $20
- SCISSORWORK by Uche Nduka, 150 pp. $20
- THIEF OF HEARTS by Maxwell Owen Clark, 116 pp. $20
- DOG DAY ECONOMY by Ted Rees, 138 pp. $20
- THE NERVE EPISTLE by Sarah Riggs, 110 pp. $20
- QUANUNDRUM: [i will be your many angled thing] by Edwin Torres, 128 pp. $20
- FETAL POSITION by Holly Melgard, 110 pp. $20
- DEATH & DISASTER SERIES by Lonely Christopher, 192 pp. $20

Roof Books are published by
Segue Foundation
For a complete listing of Roof Books, go to: roofbbooks.com
Roof Books are distributed by
Independent Publishers Group/IPGbook.com